JUNE 18, 1988

PURCHASED AT THE BRIT-RAIL STATION

SALISBURY, ENGLAND

TO CHAD FROM JOHN & CHRIS

D1616231

MEMORIES AROUND
STEAM SHEDS

Raymond Keeley

LONDON

IAN ALLAN LTD

First published 1985

ISBN 0 7110 1422 1

Published by Ian Allan Ltd, Shepperton, Surrey; and printed by Ian Allan Printing Ltd at their works at Coombelands in Runnymede, England

Left:
A GC/LNER 'ancient' relegated! One of Trafford Park's Class 'J10' locomotives acts as station pilot at Manchester Central: No 65186 is preparing to remove empty stock with Stanier No 42448 behind. *Raymond Keeley*

Below:
Revolving Stage 'West Country' class No 34012 Launceston makes use of the shed turntable at Weymouth on 6 September 1966. The absence of smokebox numberplate and nameplate will be noted. *Stewart Blencowe collection*

NOTICE
ALL ENGINES MUST STOP BEFORE COMING ON THIS TURNTABLE

Front cover, top:
Newton Heath, 5 October 1958 – left to right: Horwich Moguls Nos 42705 and 42856; 'Jubilee' No 45642 *Boscawen.* *Raymond Keeley*
Front cover, bottom:
Haymarket, the repair workshop on 21 May 1957 showing Class D30 No 62422 *Caleb Balderstone* **and No 62420** *Dominie Sampson.*
Raymond Keeley
Back cover, top:
Eastleigh Shed, May 1953. Ex-Urie/Maunsell 'H15' 4-6-0 No 30477.
Stewart Blencowe collection
Back cover, bottom:
West Hartlepool on 21 May 1958. The 'J72s' were remarkable in being constructed over a period of 54 years practically without alteration.
Raymond Keeley

Contents

Introduction

You may well think that the title *Steam Shed Magic* somewhat exaggerates the reality of what a majority of people would probably see as a drab working environment long associated with human toil and sweat. Yet it is a paradox of so many human situations that 'one man's meat is another man's poison'; clearly, it is not a matter of what we see but how we see it. In this case, or course, it revolves around the peculiar quality that pervades the whole being of the steam locomotive and impregnates the very bricks and mortar of its living quarters.

It seems that, though many of us were hooked in the days when we were young and steam was commonplace, the very familiarity effectively masked the power and potency of this peculiar quality. But when steam was near to death, the power engulfed both those of us who had grown up with it and the legions of a newer generation, who decided it must not be allowed to die.

What, you may well ask, is this 'peculiar quality'? Well I will use the word 'romance' – for it is through the romance there comes the magic. One dictionary definition (Collins) perfectly sums up romance as, 'a mysterious, exciting, sentimental or nostalgic quality'. The steam locomotive does, I think, capture each of our emotional responses that are influenced by that definition. Thus enslaved we must succumb to its charms.

Most of my generation were weaned on books with titles that laid emphasis on the mystique, the allure of railway travel and locomotives – *The Wonder Book of Railways, Track of the Royal Scot, Locos of the Royal Road,* etc. *Meccano Magazine* and *Hornby Book of Trains* helped significantly, and I for one give thanks that the sense of awe these old titles engendered has lodged imovable in one corner of my mind and that, for all the sophistication of our modern times, those who seek to preserve or photograph, or both, the steam locomotive, seem equally enthralled when in its presence.

Perhaps our immediate association of the word 'magic' is with a fairytale/folklore world of childhood and pantomime, a world of wonder and innocence. Yet, without doubt, there was an aura of magic contained within the interior of a steam shed despite the grime and industrial gloom. Perhaps it was because this sometimes semi-twilight world jangled chords of distant childhood memory; of fears and excitement; of shadows and substance in a darkened street, garden or bedroom. The remembered terror and innocence of youth mingled in the vast simmering shapes looming over the adult man making his way up and down their darkened ranks.

In three of the chapters within this volume I have endeavoured to convey something of the atmosphere and emotional appeal of the steam shed as seen by an enthusiast: if you like, the outsider looking in. In the remaining two chapters I have tried to see two particular sheds of my aquaintance against their working and, in some aspects, their social/topographical background.

Once again I am indebted to a few friends for providing assistance with suitable photographs.

Above:
'A mysterious or extraordinary quality' – sunshine attempts to pierce the dark corners of Dunfermline shed, bringing a touch of the spectral to LNER Class 'D30' No 62442 *Simon Glover* **on 22 May 1957.** *Raymond Keeley*

To Alan Blencowe – some friendships help to bring a sort of luminous quality to life which can never be fully measured. To his son Stewart, very talented in his own right as a photographer, as the various slide shows of his work that I have been privileged to attend bear witness. At present he is deeply involved, along with a few other diehards, in restoring another 'Manor' to accompany *Erlestoke*. The finished product is like seeing the tip of the iceberg, for the great mass of sheer hard work and dedication that goes on 'behind the scenes' of such projects, is below the surface.

Once again nothing has been too much trouble for Gordon Coltas in searching his collection for suitable prints. His is the kindly obliging sort of spirit it is a pleasure to be in contact with.

I must also mention Mr John Fozard of Shipley. His expertise in processing from negative to print has transformed many of my more difficult negatives. Sometimes he produces results I would hardly have believed possible. Long may he continue to provide such a service.

Lastly the 'Raymond Keeley collection' type of prints. These trouble me greatly mainly because I am anxious to give credit to the expertise of these unknown (to me) photographers. They did such a great job, but it is not always possible to identify them. I can only feel humbly grateful that they were in the right place at the right time and hope that by showing a wider audience the results of their labour there is some compensation.

Raymond Keeley
Stockport

1 Steam Shed Magic

. . . casting the spell!

MAGIC!
Consider for a moment how evocative the word is: so short, but so full of meaning, vibrating with significance like ripples from a stone that slips unseen into a pool of dark water.

A favourite dictionary definition of the word has it 'a mysterious or extraordinary quality'. Such a description exactly fitted the mystique – the aura of wonder, excitement and expectation of discovery – that penetrated every nook and cranny of a steam locomotive shed. Once caught you became a slave for life.

Just why steam's 'livid beast' should be so fascinating is a mystery: perhaps it is beyond human understanding how unseen strands can be gathered, and together cast a spell that holds captive our imagination. It certainly happens in so many forms of human activity – both spiritual and physical, though the physical will almost certainly be related to a stimulus of the mind.

The mystique of a steam locomotive shed, and especially that of its residents, was, and still is, ever present. Possibly this is in the memory of things that have passed beyond physical recall but remain clear in the mind's eye; or in the anticipation of visits to present day rail centres with their galaxy of preserved and pristine images in steam, now garlanded with all the colour of long ago. In whatever way we see it, it still has a seemingly timeless relevance.

I hope my writing will act as a memory sounding board for all who are captured by the sight, sounds and smell of a steam shed. You may have been converted long ago when almost every district of a large town or city had its own loco shed or depot; or you may be one of the young or older enthusiasts (in this activity the generation gap seems to make no difference) who always feel a quiver of excitement when passing through those large doors at Carnforth, Dinting, Didcot or the host of today's sheds.

Visiting a locomotive shed in the heyday of steam was a highly emotive experience guaranteed to bring a quickening of the pulse. It didn't matter what time of day or night it was; indeed, as I have described later in the book, a night visit could be even more charged with atmosphere. The visit might be to a remote shed in some distant corner of Britain, or the local one a five-minute bike ride away, but it made no difference; familiar or not the magic still remained.

The emotional lift is still there in the 1980s, though the feeling now is perhaps more related to a pilgrimage, an opening of doors to reveal a past glory. Each of these remaining places is Mecca for a multitude who come to watch and browse. The feeling is even more agonisingly poignant for those who, with great sense of achievement and satisfaction, have brought a rusting relic home to roost at Buxton or Bridgnorth, Steamport or Loughborough. Then through the pain of great labour and vast effort there is transformation, a rebirth, a reaffirmation of man's innate creativity.

I used the phrase 'visiting a locomotive shed'. That is of course strictly correct: one did go as a visitor. Yet a niggle in me says that we never visited a steam shed in the rather formal way implied; the phrase is altogether too prosaic. It doesn't convey the almost anguished thrill of anticipation that most enthusiasts would feel, especially when it was one of those huge working steam sheds that might house well in excess of 100 engines. We may have assumed a rather casual manner but this was the careful facade that cloaks the serious enthusiast's approach to his interest. It soon slipped to reveal a sense of delight if the unexpected was found hidden amidst the massed locomotive ranks. We all have our treasured memories – it might be the last unrebuilt 'Scot' to add to the 69 already 'copped', or perhaps an ex-North Eastern 4-6-0 deep in the inner recesses of Gorton. Even a Terrier at Fratton in the twilight days of steam, though not unexpected always seemed

unreal, like a manifestation of another age.

So, if 'to visit' does not sum up the experience, which verbs should be used? The answer is simple. One always proposed to 'do', or perhaps had 'done' a shed. The overtones in the words ring out clearly as a declaration of implacable intent or of trumph and achievement, that frequently concealed a deeper satisfaction.

There were several different ways of doing a shed, usually, if with a party, it was by written permit, and that was the officially correct way. But it was not always so and often I have waited in a shed foreman's office while the great man either used the phone or instructed a subordinate – all the time I would be hoping he was in a good mood. Obviously these were men who carried a burden of heavy responsibility and always they seemed to project an aura of quiet authority. They were formidable figures indeed and sometimes just a little sceptical of one's purpose. So there were tense moments when a maximum effort would be made to impress with an image of grown up care and responsibility. Even as an adult I would feel some trepidation

Below:
Steam's 'livid beasts' caged. Eastleigh shed on 24 June 1959. Southern Region's Class 'S15' No 30500 and BR Standard Class '4' No 75005 breathe and simmer, while 'Lord Nelson' class No 30855 *Robert Blake* patiently receives human attention. *Raymond Keeley*

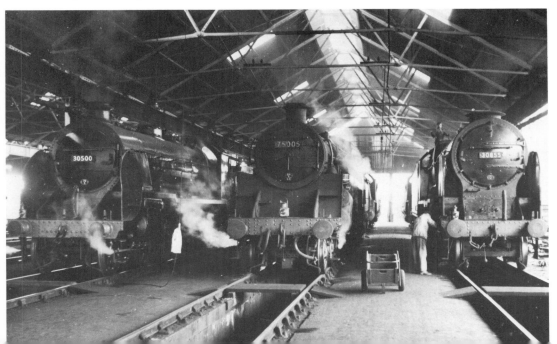

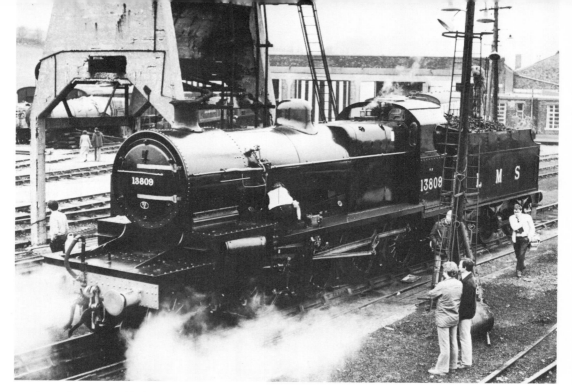

Above:
'The emotional lift is still there in the 1980s' . . .
**Carnforth on 27 March 1982. Ex-Somerset &
Dorset 2-8-0 No 13809, in superb external
condition, had just completed one leg of a
'Cumbrian Mountain Pullman' run.** *Raymond
Keeley*

and perhaps a slight sense of guilt for
disturbing such an arduous routine. My
strategy, to emphasise the serious
approach, might involve revealing a
knowledge of the particular types of
locomotive shedded there and the sort of
work they were used for; or perhaps there
may have been an opportunity to touch a
chord of rapport concerning a mutual
love for a particular locomotive type,
both long or recently departed for scrap.
In several cases of my own experience
this would reveal that the man on the
other side of the desk had fired a particular type in his youth, or driven one in
his maturity.

In this way I did strike up a much
treasured friendship with a gentleman at
Balornock (St Rollox) depot, for he had
been a fireman on those magnificent but
controversial, in terms of performance,
Pickersgill '956' class 4-6-0s. They were, in
my opinion, one of the most handsome
designs of 4-6-0 to come off any drawing
board. In absolute beauty of line they
were only rivalled, among large express
locomotives north of the border, by Reid's

legendary Atlantics and that most superb
of all large tank engines, Whitelegg's
Glasgow and South Western 4-6-4 Baltic
tanks. All three were supreme examples
of the steam locomotive builder's art. All
were destroyed at a time when we were
only just beginning to appreciate the
treasure trove of Victorian/Edwardian
elegance that in the first half of this
century surrounded us on all sides: so
much has been saved, especially in the
last 10 or 15 years, but so much has gone
beyond recall! My reverence for a class
that I had only ever seen in photographs
revealed a mutual feeling from a working
enthusiast. He had fired them in his
younger days and remembered them in
the glory of Caledonian blue. However, I
digress, more of that association later.

Above:
'Then through the pain of great labour and vast effort there is transformation'. The magnificently restored Great Western 'Manor' No 7812 *Erlestoke Manor* **double-heads a similar transformation in No 4930** *Hagley Hall* **on an enthusiasts special at Craven Arms, 24 April 1982.** *Stewart Blencowe collection*

In my wartime wanderings this attempt to find some common bond, plus the help of a blue uniform, more often than not served me well. I experienced some memorable shed trips, meeting in the process some kind, understanding people. No shed foreman can ever quite appreciate the debt of gratitude and joy one feels on these occasions, especially if his answer had been 'aye, all right then, but watch your step and report to me on the way out!'.

Young men, with their greater sense of adventure – and boldness! – are often prepared to try things that older people would like to do but lack the drive. Often therefore, it was a case of 'who dares wins'! On sleepy Saturday afternoons

when, for most of the youth of my day, the sound and uproar of life was concentrated around the football or cricket fields, then an infinitely more enchanting sound, like the siren call of the sea nymphs of old, lured me and I was summoned to the places where locomotives seemed to slumber quietly in their lairs.

Sometimes other, quieter places called – a favourite embankment, perhaps; a secret grassy place vibrant with the sound of bird life and nature, distanced from the move discordant mortal world. It required a patient wait for different sounds; a slight tremor in the earth that brought a quickening of the anticipation. What would it be? Perhaps a 'Sandringham', gorgeously arrayed in apple green – at at that time, they were indeed the apple of my eye. It might be *Hinchinbrooke* or *Somerleyton Hall*, both old friends and frequently seen. But some distance away in the long shallow curve of the cutting, a high column of smoke and steam against the southern sky suggested something working much harder and approaching at a slower and more deliberate pace than would be expected from a passenger train. Sure enough the coal black but formidable image that burst from under the nearby overbridge was a superb 'B7', swathed in a halo of white steam, masculine and mighty of chest. No other engine of my then aquaintance had such an indomit-áble, purposeful look to its smokebox face, and the attributes were fully born out in practice and performance. The sight of such a great engine moving, with turbulent furore, its lengthy goods train towards the distant Hyde Road station was like an intoxicating balm to my soul.

But whatever did appear, the quietly expectant atmosphere would, for a few brief moments, shatter to a thundering extrovert sound – all the more potent for the contrast with the quiet natural sigh of the air and creatures around. On such occasions some of us lived life with a heady exhilaration – a feeling that can sometimes be relived today in the pursuit of preserved steam. (Ironically the parti-cular spot to which I made some of my jaunts in the mid-1930, would, a year or two hence, be gouged away to make room for a new repair and maintenance depot. A future electric traction dream that, in so short a time, is already a memory!)

The choice available to me at that time must be hard to imagine today. I lived but a short bike ride from the great complex at Gorton; near also to what some might claim an equal attraction – Longsight and, nearby a main line to Euston. As an alternative to open air delights, therefore, the bike might be pointed towards one of those places where the 'livid beasts' found rest from toil.

It was a solitary pursuit – and because of that seemed much more daring. I cannot imagine any big game hunter stalking his quarry found greater thrill as, with stealth, one quickly tiptoed round gloomy depths entering magical names

Below:
'Even a "Terrier" at Fratton in the twilight days of steam' – Fratton was the home shed for these dainty little engines when they worked the Hayling Island branch. No 32646 rests between duties on 28 August 1958. *Raymond Keeley*

and numbers in grimy notebooks. Gorton and Longsight were, in a sense, impregnable, but there were one or two lesser places where it was occasionally possible to see a part of the shed's complement of steam. It required quiet care and manoeuvre: but never with thought of harm. That would have been quite unthinkable for these were our gods of steam – their place of repose was as much a hallowed dwelling as any cathedral and always treated as such.

Occasionally, when confronted by an uncompromising authority, there was sad retreat leaving a conviction that an elusive Compound, 'Director', 'Precursor' or some lesser breed, had been almost within the grasp. But sometimes, when the disappointment was all too apparent,

Below:
Sunderland shed on 21 May 1958 with LNER Class 'A8' 4-6-2 tanks Nos 69878 and 69855 and the author with his Ensign held ready. The gloom of a straight line shed could pose great problems for the photographer. *Alan Blencowe*

there would be a kindly hand on the shoulder to guide one quickly round. On these occasions appreciation in the form of 'Oh thank you mister' came from the heart!

Today the situation is quite different, the shed doors are open and the multitude who pay their dues are welcomed. No longer is the visitor a potential disturber of busy routines; he or she have become the life blood, the prime reason for the preservation of the steam scene and without whose contributions the herculean efforts of the volunteers would be in jeopardy.

Since locomotive sheds were, in the main, usually located in built up or industrialised areas the entrance ways to most were, to say the least, unprepossessing. Sometimes it would be through a narrow gateway in a high fence constructed of thick balks of wood – a sort of outer ring of defence. This would, in some cases, lead on to a footbridge then a sleepered pathway across a maze of lines. I lifted the latch of such gateways many times at places as far apart as Longsight

and Eastfield. At the former, as a somewhat timid schoolboy, I never achieved more than the first few steps up the footbridge – though even from that vantage point one had a splendid view of the main line and some comings and goings from the shed. Eastfield was a different proposition, mainly I think because it came later when I was in my early 20s and wearing the 'open sesame' of a blue uniform.

A quite different sort of approach way to the citadel (some of the larger sheds had a somewhat daunting, fortress like, presence, at least so it seemed to me as a young boy in the mid-1930s) could see you confronted by a large double gateway in a brick wall that perhaps opened onto a cobbled roadway. On crossing the threshold you would be frowned upon by faded brick buildings of threatening appearance – and there may have been some distance to go before arriving at the shed proper.

Most sheds of my later acquaintance were possessed of a motley collection of small dusty-windowed outbuildings, silted round the edges with dirt or sickly looking soil which had lodged in crevices between brick and cobbles where sooted grass and weed made vain attempt to grow – nature's efforts to arrest the inroads of man. What these outbuildings housed was anybody's guess – oil stores, lamps, bikes, or, perhaps, the rusting bones of a thousand nuts, bolts, levers and countless other smaller parts of a locomotive's innards. Such places were the expected 'props' at any shed – part of the backstage setting from which those most glamorous performers ventured forth into the footlight glare of performance. Extroverts all, they were so ready to entertain and we, the converted, could hardly wait to applaud.

An occasional glimpse into one of these buildings through an open door

Above:
'and every one an Aladdin's Cave!'... Darlington roundhouse, 21 May 1958. From left to right, 'J72' No 68679, 'A5' No 69840, 'J50' No 68897 and 'A8' No 69887. The particular interest of this photograph is that it shows four ultimates. The 'J72' and 'J50' represent the final development of the 0-6-0T on the North Eastern and Great Northern Railways respectively. The 'A5' type, designed by Robinson, was the Great Central Railway's last design of large passenger tank engine. The 'A8' was, in a sense, an extension of Vincent Raven's very unusual design of 4-4-4T for the North Eastern Railway, being rebuilt in LNER days to a more conventional form of 4-6-2T. *Raymond Keeley*

would perhaps reveal a brick-walled room covered in brown wracked whitewash, looking like the interior of a dungeon. The contents might consist of a rather primitive wooden table, a collection of rickety chairs and, often prominent in such rest rooms, one of those long narrow wooden forms, the knots and crevices of wood grain on the shiny seat polished smooth by long years of contact with serge-trousered human seats. On the table might be the odd chipped 'billy can' a few brown pot mugs and some screwed up sandwich wrapping paper. Hovering in the background of the better endowed of such rooms would be the heavy blackened gas stove, complete with brown earthenware teapot and aluminium kettle.

Do I seem to paint a rather bleak picture? Man, right down the ages, has always been the most resourceful of creatures when it comes to finding comfort and homeliness in the most austere surroundings. Doubtless such places could offer a brief respite from the daily grind and, though spartan in terms of both comfort and those facilities for refreshing the inner man, must have provided a very acceptable haven for tired men working long, physically arduous, hours.

The outer areas of a shed may well have appeared a little unkempt and dreary, even somewhat forbidding, but such an approach seemed entirely right for entering the domain of the most earthy of man's mechanical creations. They served,

13

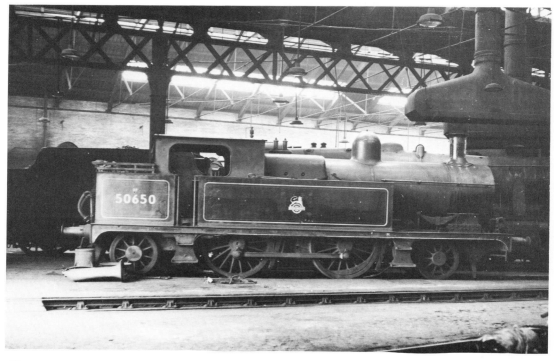

Above:
'Joys of the unexpected'
Wellingborough 22 July 1956 showing an L&Y 2-4-2T deep in the heart of Midland territory. No 50650 was for a short time spare engine for the Higham Ferrers Branch. One wonders at times how some of the more unlikely transfers in steam days came about – though it even happens in the present day. I certainly never expected to see Class 45 diesels in regular use on the North Wales main line, but they were there in 1983 and doubtless there are good operational reasons. It certainly creates a constant interest for the enthusiast. *Stewart Blencowe collection*

in a way, to quicken the pulse and under-line a deep feeling of anticipation – a sense of being on the threshold! The entrance to a main shed building lacked the regal splendour of oak pannelled doors and brass handles. Indeed they were quite the reverse: many entrances, in my experience, were through rather battered looking inconspicuous doorways in the outer wall. They seemed – to my vivid imagination like the heavy, locked and mysterious doorways, one might come across in the seclusion of the cloistered close of a cathedral: those which must lead to a sacred inner sanctum. The ancient paintwork would be rubbed and bruised at the edges by countless thousands of heavy booted feet, yet no magic casement ever revealed a more captivating treasure. The first view into the darkened interior was always breathtaking whether through being confronted by a grimy 6 ft 9 in driving wheel topped by an alluring nameplate, or a row of tender ends and smokebox doors; all were evidence of the delights awaiting in the smokey gloom.

The main building of a shed housing the locomotive complement, large or small, was usually plain and architec-turally modest. Yet it is hard to imagine that any other sort of brick-walled, slate and glass-roofed space could contain so much dirt, grime, smoke and dust, but at the same time so much seductive charm. Theirs was a power to bewitch and excite far beyond the imagination of those not

Above:
Fire Queen in the deep slumber of six decades, May 1949. The engine had been entombed in her tiny shed at Llanberis, on the Dinorwic Slate Quarries Railway, since 1886. She would remain there until 1969 when, restored to former glory, she was removed to the excellent Penryn Locomotive Museum. The photograph demonstrates the extremely cramped conditions which could sometimes confront the photographer! *Raymond Keeley*

addicted, and every one was an Alladin's cave.

No matter how many times one entered, the eyes could feast themselves on a treasure trove. It might just consist of old friends with perhaps the occasional unexpected addition, or alternatively a whole chestful of new jewels. So many occasions come to mind, occasions when no genie with a magic lamp could have better fulfilled my most earnest wishes – the surprise of finding that Metropolitan tank quietly resting at the back of Lincoln shed in April 1942 (LNER Class 'H2' No 6420) or the unexpected discovery of *Fire Queen* in the deep slumber of six decades, in her tiny shed at the Dinorwic Slate Quarries, Llanberis (1949).

Once inside, the dark of these walls gathered you to a bosom that was magic indeed. For these, no matter how humble, were the palaces of Kings (and not just the Western variety!). Whatever claims we may make in the present day for being captured by the paraphernalia of the railways – the stations, viaducts, signal-boxes, locomotive sheds, carriage stock or pre- and post-group vintage – there can be little doubt that we clutch at these as one might the picture frame from which the picture has faded almost to vanishing point. They provided the scenery for a stage upon which strode the live performers – the real stars of our affection. Without the actors even the most brilliantly effective stage setting, which may in its own right have great artistic merit, will hardly spring vividly to life and captivating movement.

In the 1970s and 80s it has been the lot

of the big diesel and electric locomotives to stride that stage and, if not with quite the costume, colour and character of the steam locomotive, they have at least provided a focusing point. They represent the traditional power unit quite separate from and at the head of a rake of carriages or freight wagons and, in the case of the diesel locomotive, can produce quite magical exhaust sounds. What enthusiast could mistake the highly individual atmospheric sound of a 'Whistler', or the tearaway excitement of the low key 'Deltic' scream? I remember a few years ago at the beginning of a North Wales holiday – in the days when S0 holiday extras and reliefs were a little more prolific than nowadays – the expected Stoke–Llandudno eight-coach DMU had departed well filled from Crewe. Then, to my delight, the authorities decided to run a duplicate stopping at Chester and the main coast resorts as far as Llandudno Junction. This turned up in the form of half a dozen elderly open coaches hauled by a Class 25. We had at least half of the first coach to ourselves. It was a warm day and, with all the windows open, the sound of the '25' came loud and clear – just like the soft shoe shuffle of an 'A4' at 70mph, I said to my wife, though I think any subtlety in the remark eluded her. Certainly, with half closed eyes and the imagination at work, that '25' at 40mph was providing a quite notable and respectable impersonation of one of Gresley's wonderful Pacifics.

Several of the diesels have so endeared themselves to us that even the most hardened steam buff would, I am sure, admit to at least one favourite. For myself it has to be the Class 40s, as evidenced by the number of times they currently appear in my camera viewfinder. Names have

Below:
Dinting 28 March 1982. Thirty years ago in a heyday of steam, I could never in my wildest dreams have imagined finding such an old fashioned looking shed scene 30 years hence. Even less could I have expected such a scene to contain a North Western 'Jumbo' and a 'Coal Tank', both in working condition and standing in the yard leading into a diminutive Great Central shed! *Raymond Keeley*

helped quite significantly, witness the 'Westerns', 'Deltics' etc; and latterly platform end life at Euston, Crewe, Manchester, Piccadilly and all the rest have been the livelier for the blue-backed red nameplates of the electrics. Here, in the northwest, where we are entertained by the growl and whistle of the '40s', the railway scene will be distinctly the poorer when they finally go.

If we are to judge from the legacy passed on by the earlier railway photographers it was the express train in motion that rivetted their attention. Above all it was the steam locomotive in full cry that epitomised to the full every bit of the glamour and allure of this living, breathing creation of man. Once hooked, it compelled them to return time and time again – for which we remain indebted. It was an aphrodisiac whose potency and heady effect enslaved two or three generations when steam was still the workhorse; those, who – with prodigious energy – stumbled about sometimes weighed down with cumbersome but effective plate cameras to get the record for posterity. The hypnotic attraction is still there, and with increasing effect now that the preserved animal has become a prima donna to be cosseted and fussed over – long may it last!

Though steam in action had this mesmeric effect, its appeal was more often an almost physical thing. If we silently cheered, from the lineside, it was as a result of the sort of appeal that makes the crowd roar when the home side scores, or when the odds against outsider is first past the winning post. Our blood surged and the nerve ends tingled as the smoke and steam billowed around and we caught the exhilarating rear threequarter view of a 'Green Arrow', straining in every metallic

Below:
I cannot resist including this photograph of a favourite class of Great Central 4-6-0. It is a long way from my location mentioned in the text yet there is an affinity, the engine is clearly on a lengthy goods and the late 1930s was a time I remember them so well in the Manchester/Sheffield area. Class 'B7' No 5469 seen near Staverton Road, June 1939. *Gordon Coltas*

sinew as it launched its long heavy train from the Grantham stop towards Stoke Tunnel. Or perhaps it was a 'Duchess', battling away at the barrier of Shap, shouting with a mighty voice that echoed across the bleak windswept fells – an indomitable battering ram forcing hilltop ramparts.

Steam on shed – at home – was different, though no less captivating. The emotions were still aflame, though it was likely to be more a direct appeal to the intellect. Perhaps there are Freudian overtones: the dark cosiness; being physically close to the beast despite all the dirt and smoke; the perpetual twilight gloom, almost designed to conceal treasured items until the last moment, something akin to the hide and seek joys of childhood and adding greatly to the overall mystique.

The great variety in shed locations helped considerably to give the imprint of character and depended on a number of factors that to a large extent determined shape and layout. Availability of land, especially if in a built up area, was a major influence. As far as possible a shed would have to be strategically placed to serve most economically the needs of routes and services to be operated; thus it

'Without the actors – even the most brilliantly effective stage setting, which may in its own right have great artistic merit, will hardly spring vividly to life and captivating movement'.

Above:
A Leading Man Prepares LNER Class 'A2' No 60539 *Bronzino* **at new England depot 16 August 1958. Note the overhead water cranes for servicing each road simultaneously.** *Alan Blencowe*

would usually be required adjacent to major junctions, large centres of heavy industry and the major railway stations, though land availability sometimes caused them to be built some distance away from the areas they served. It was possible to find large sheds in the heart of the country and, paradoxically, some quite small ones in heavily built up and industrialised areas.

Many sheds, during the course of their lifetime, became ultimately part of an urban pattern of development, though when originally built they may well have been the first major intrusion into a semi-rural landscape. This became very apparent during the interwar years that saw the first great outward surge of many

towns and cities into the surrounding countryside. Thus, though most steam sheds are part of past history, the areas they occupied influenced, and remain an influence, on the shape of whole communities. It is a situation that will remain well into the foreseeable future, no matter whether the areas remain as grassy scrubland or become part of industrial or housing development.

To recall just a few locations is sufficient to emphasise the many and seemingly infinite variations one could expect in the enchanting world of the steam locomotive shed.

It was possible for a shed and yards to be totally surrounded by ribbons of steel rail, as at Didcot, yet still have a countrified air. Or it might seem completely engulfed in a Victorian industrialised gloom, with rails, blast furnaces and steel mills seeming to stretch as far as the eye could see. Such a place, in the Valley of the River Don between Sheffield and Rotherham, had the appropriate name of Grimesthorpe, with, in the halcyon days, a tram stop at the gates and a grandstand view of shed yards from the upper deck. To me that place, where even a blade of grass had to struggle for existence, was quite idyllic, and that may seem a paradox. Yet if one accepts that the green and watery surface of our planet sits upon a raging inferno in its bowels that can appeal to a darker side of our imagination, then Grimesthorpe was a man-made imitation. Satanic mills abounded, and here, at the heart of it all, revelling in the sulphuric atmosphere, the fiery monarch who captures us with Mephistophelian, hypnotic charm!

Liverpool's Brunswick was something of a witch's cauldron, cramped in a black hole with frowning sandstone cliffs as a backdrop. March – well you could say it was in the country and probably within earshot of marsh birds and the night cries of other wild life, though it did stand on the shore of a veritable sea of railway lines, the vast marshalling yards at Whitemoor. Mighty Crewe North – just across a footbridge at the north end of the station platforms – nestled snugly in the

curve of the Chester and North Wales line. It had heard the thunder of all those giants of the Premier Line – the 'Georges', 'Precursors' and 'Claughtons' – then played host to the lean debonair racers with the Stanier profile. Crewe is as busy as ever but North Shed is a grey shaled wasteland looking pathetically small in area, as does any open space after a large imposing building has been demolished. But – and the mind boggles – however did such a small space house so many giants? Tiny and secret Penmaenpool, only room for a couple of engines, but in later days, with the haunting shades of Great Westernry and the ever present scenic backdrop of Cader Idris, to say nothing of the breathtaking Mawddach Estuary in the foreground, there were compensations indeed.

If the catalogue of main line steam sheds seemed almost endless, even in the days of the 1950s one could probably double the total with the addition of those on colliery and other industrial lines. They occupied a world of their own pervaded by its own special enchantment. In most cases the sheds were quite small with space for perhaps only two or three

engines, but resident in some of sheds, usually aged and perhaps tired in the limbs, could be found some real gems in the form of discarded engines from the main line companies. Some became so celebrated that they were the cause of many a lengthy pilgrimage by enthusiasts. They usually worked alongside examples of those legions of compact and very neat small tank engine types produced by locomotive building companies, whose names now sound like something from railway folklore and who specialised in small industrial locomotives.

Would you believe that with such a surfeit of riches there could be a problem? But indeed such did exist, for in those days there was just too much to see and fully take in, and for the enthusiast with normal domestic commitments it was virtually impossible to do full justice to more than a small fraction.

Member of the Chorus GWR 0-4-2T No 1438 at Oswestry on 25 June 1961. This was a type introduced by Collet in 1932 for branch line work. *Raymond Keeley*

Veteran Performer St Rollox Works May 1957 showing one of Dugald Drummond's little 0-4-0 saddle tanks built for the Caledonian Railway in 1900 in immaculate condition as works shunter 57 years later. What a gem for preservation – but sad to say she was scrapped in 1960! *Raymond Keeley*

'For myself it has to be the Class 40s'

Left:
An unidentified Class 40 on the 8.48 SO Manchester Piccadilly – Skegness passing New Mills station on 21 September 1976. The partially lifted lines leading off to the right of the picture enter a tunnel on the one time Hayfield Branch (now lifted). This short section is now a dead end for stabling DMUs on local Piccadilly–New Mills service. *Raymond Keeley*

Below:
Stockport on 9 August 1975 Class 40 No. 40.186 is standing at platform 3 facing north, having brought in the 3.22pm Blackpool–Euston train. A collision between two goods trains at Weaver Junction on 6 September 1975 caused severe disruption on the West Coast main line. Hence No 40.186 brought the train from Warrington to Stockport, an electric locomotive then being coupled at the opposite end allowing it once again to head, via Crewe, in the direction of Euston. Driver Pomeroy of Warrington, stands at the cab door of an immaculate locomotive. *Raymond Keeley*

Right:
Class No 40.035 leaving Bangor west tunnel with the 16.55 Holyhead–Manchester train on 21 September 1974. The splendid castellated overbridge at the station is clearly framed.
Raymond Keeley

'Above all it was the steam locomotive in full cry that epitomised to the full every bit of the glamour, the allure of this living breathing creation of man –'

Below:
The Tilbury line in 1935. I just had to find a reason for including this splendid, evocative photograph of Ted Brightmans. It shows 4-4-2T No 2147 on an Ealing–Southend train. This Whitelegg tank engine from a turn of the century design, was originally LTSR No 79 *Rippleside.* The original LMS number was 2176, renumbering to 2147 in 1930. the LTSR corridor stock will be noted. *E. Brightman via Stewart Blencowe*

Bottom:
Down fitted freight passing Leighton Buzzard on 8 February 1960 with 'Royal Scot' No 46120 *Royal Inniskilling Fusilier* in charge. *Alan Blencowe*

Left:

I have no information concerning the location of this shot or the photographer. I imagine that the absence of smoke deflectors on the engine – 'Lord Nelson' No 858 *Lord Duncan* – puts it around 1929–30 and the type of stock suggests it to be a boat train. But that sort of conjecture apart, the photograph, at least as I see it, must be one of the best ever 'action' shots of a 'Nelson'!
Raymond Keeley collection

Below left:

A mid-1930s excursion, probably Blackpool into West Yorkshire, on Sowerby Bridge troughs. The diminutive engine – at least in comparison to the carriage stock – is No 12279, one of the small but sturdy Aspinall 0-6-0s built in 1895 for the Lancashire & Yorkshire Railway. It is a type I normally associated with light goods work and, in the 1940s and 50s, with the Miles Platting banking stint. I photographed them many times in the late 1950s while standing on the banking road adjacent to platform 12 at Manchester Victoria (see *Memories of LMS Steam*). The very lively picture shows that these elderly looking little engines still had plenty of life when given a chance to show their paces. *Gordon Coltas*

Below:

Down express headed by Class 'A4' No 60017 *Silver Fox* passing Walton (north of Peterborough) on 14 August 1954. Its a superb shot of an 'A4' getting into its stride to tackle Stoke Bank, with at least 14, possibly more, coaches behind the tender. The pronounced 'bow' of the third coach will be noted; also the ex-LMS Leicester lines to the right of the picture.
Alan Blencowe

'Steam on shed – at home was different, though no less captivating'

Left:
Ex-LNWR 2-4-0 No 790 *Hardwicke* at Carnforth on 9 May 1976. I had an article in the October 1976 issue of *Railway Magazine,* which outlines the events of that very special day. *Raymond Keeley*

Below:
No 6906 *Chicheley Hall* standing against the coaling stage at Banbury depot in the late 1950s. *Stewart Blencowe collection*

Bottom:
Ex-LMS Class '2P' 4-4-0 No 40538 at Millhouses Shed in the 1950s. The engine, which is a rebuild of a late 19th century Johnson design for the Midland Railway, has over half a century of hard working life behind her. *Stewart Blencowe collection*

Above:
Cambridge on 13 April 1957. Though perhaps one could be forgiven for seeing No 61616 *Falloden* as a Gresley 'Sandringham', she in fact appears as a two-cylinder rebuild by Edward Thompson and classified as 'B2'. *Alan Blencowe*

Below:
'A tram stop at the gates!' Sheffield (Grimesthorpe) winter 1932. This and the following print show engines on the 'outside' turntable. Horwich Mogul No 13138 carrys a shed plate numbered 25 denoting Sheffield. The code predates the LMS being an original number for the shed in Midland days. So far as I am able to ascertain the oval form of shedplate, now so familiar was an original Midland innovation dating from around the turn of the century.
Gordon Coltas

Above:
Sheffield (Grimesthorpe), winter 1932. Midland Compound No 1091 was one of the standard LMS variety, being built in 1925. The engine also carrys the shed code 25. *Gordon Coltas*

They occupied a world of their own pervaded by its own special enchantment.

Below:
Lea Green Colliery (Near St Helens Lancs.) on 22 May 1959. *Bellerophon,* an outside cylinder 0-6-0 well tank built by Richard Evans & Co of Haydock: this exquisite unique design of locomotive was built in 1874 and withdrawn from service in 1964. Like so many small industrial locomotives this one worked in comparative obscurity throughout its life. Fortunately it escaped the cutter's torch and is now preserved on the Keighley and Worth Valley Railway. *Raymond Keeley*

Above:
A long way from its birthplace at the Longhedge Works of the London Chatham and Dover Railway in 1879, this little 0-6-0T stands in the works yard at the National Coal Boards workshops at Haydock (St Helens area). Though it had worked in this area for a number of years it still, by a quirk of fate, carries its old Southern Railway number! *Raymond Keeley*

Below:
Aberaman (About two miles north of Mountain Ash, South Wales), where NCB 0-6-0ST *Sir John* (Avonside 1914) finds a makeshift water supply while working near the phurnacite plant at Aberaman. *Raymond Keeley*

Above:
NCB Walkden works yard on 23 September 1958. Two of the ex-North Stafford 0-6-2Ts bought from the LMS by the then Manchester Collieries before the war. The names *King George VI* (foreground) and *Kenneth* (behind) were bestowed by the new owners. *Raymond Keeley*

Below:
Walkden Yard again, 21 May 1959. 0-6-0ST *Colonel* (Hunslet Engine Co 1927) receives some attention to his 'innards'. *Raymond Keeley*

2 Cheshire Lines Twins – 1

Costume, colour and pagentry have always been – and indeed still are – things that the British enjoy. This can be seen everywhere from the opulent splendour of 'Trouping the Colour', in what is perhaps the most beguiling capital city of the Western world for displays of pomp and circumstance, to the numerous events round the country like carnivals, whit walks, vintage vehicle rallies etc. All bring out the peacock finery of dress or the paintpot giltwork to gild the lily of aged ironwork in train, traction engine, tram and bus.

The 19th and early 20th centuries saw this love of splendour – hitherto more closely associated with the patriotic belief in national supremity and destiny – mirrored in the railway companies best summed up as a passionate 'pride in the line'. This period saw intense rivalries between different railways at all levels,

from boards of directors down to the porter with his trolley.

It is doubtful if the boardrooms reflected altruistic views, and certainly in the parliamentary battles it was a matter of establishing areas of physical dominance and thus spheres of commercial autonomy, the rivalry being concerned

Below:
The map shows the position of Trafford Park shed (extreme lower left) in relation to Cornbrook carriage sidings and Central station. The Bridgewater Canal threads its way across the middle of the map towards its terminal basin at Cornbrook. To the west a large section of the vast Manchester Ship Canal/Trafford Park industrial complex can be seen. It could be said that the two and a half square mile area represented the hub of 19th century industrial expansion in Manchester. But that massive leap forward which, in the case of the Ship Canal, saw great cargo liners steam into the centre of Manchester, is now fast becoming part of a past age of sea transport.

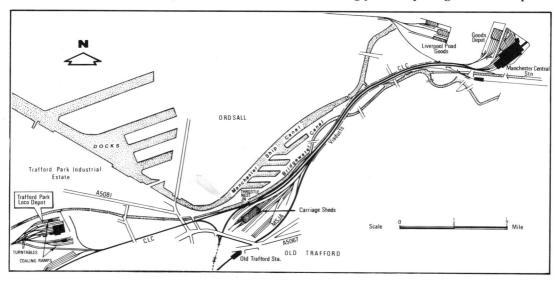

with the building of business empires and the creation of wealth.

There was a world of difference at the lower levels inhabited by men of a simple yet perhaps more fundamental and less complex scale of values, men deeply, inherently, imbued with a sense of the dignity of labour. For them it became an expression of that much maligned but never the less admirable facet of the human psyche – pride! Pride – in the name and gold braid around the peaked caps that they wore with such dignity; Pride – in the coat of arms or initials on a locomotive cab side or tender, or in lettering carved deep in the stonework of a station facade. When the letters spelt just one word – EUSTON – and they graced a massive Doric portico, even the name of the railway became over-shadowed, since any employee passing beneath that facade knew that this indeed was the 'Premier Line'.

Yet there were apparent incongruities to this rivalry, examples of congenial – or what seemed congenial – partnerships that to all intents defied the laws of logic. In particular it seemed that there existed on some of the joint lines of Britain a sort of intense brotherhood that, despite joint ownership, equalled anything to be found on single company lines. The reason was, I imagine, that although jointly owned they were really quite separate railways – well almost! If, for example, you worked on the Somerset & Dorset Line, I do not imagine your allegiance would bend in the slightest towards the parent companies, even though the locomotives were pure Midland in style. The joint lines may have operated under two flags, but they fluttered sufficiently high to be out of sight of those below. This was thwarted, intentionally or otherwise, that dark enigmatic foible in the human character which encourages a reactionary competitive spirit. At its most mild it says 'our engines are bigger, better, more powerful than yours' – the 'us and them' syndrome. At its worst the overtones are more sinister and a difference of uniform or club colours is a possible cause for verbal or physical assault.

On the railways of Britain in pre-nationalisation days there were many area of joint operation, where running lines, stations, sheds and the other paraphernalia of the railway were used by more than one company. The degree of this joint working could vary considerably. It may have been just a few miles of track or a station that for reasons of geographical convenience was used by more

The approach to Manchester Central

Below:
No 46158 *The Loyal Regiment* **on the 1 in 100 approach to Manchester Central with the 7.5am from Buxton on 6 May 1961. Sadly, this one-time Midland line alternative for Buxton–Manchester commuters was swept away in the holocaust of the 1960s. Lines to the left in the picture are those between Manchester Pondon Road and Altrincham.** *Raymond Keeley*

than one company. In pre-Grouping days there were several quite large jointly owned or worked stations with working practices that in some cases survived well into the era of British Railways. Indeed the remnants of such practice, as they concern the part of a station used by certain services, survive in one or two cases to this day. At the other end of the spectrum were railways, which although jointly owned, dominated large areas of the country with their own staff, locomotives, operating/management boards etc.

The Cheshire Lines was one of the three great joint railway systems of Britain (the others being the Somerset & Dorset Joint and the Midland & Great Northern Joint) with many of its own distinguishing features. In one particular it differed quite radically from the other two in that it did not use its own locomotives, and possibly because of this there did not seem quite that distinctive pride in the line one sensed in the other two. The S&D and the M&GN, perhaps because they were railways with a considerable rural aspect, achieved an almost 'enclosed order', where a small family atmosphere survived virtually to the time of nationalisation.

The Cheshire Lines also differed from the other two in that its 'main line'

connected the two major conurbations of the northwest. In pre-Group days the cities of Liverpool and Manchester were connected by three very competitive railway routes. The London & North Western, using George Stephenson's original Manchester–Liverpool line of 1830, was the meat in the sandwich with the Cheshire Lines running almost parallel but some miles to the south and the Lancashire & Yorkshire making something of a shallow arching curve to the north. The London & North Western's West Coast main line bisected the apex of the curve at the northern platform edges of Wigan North Western station. The Lancashire & Yorkshire made every effort to reduce the disadvantage of distance, by flattening out the curve in a couple of places and, at all times, using the most elite of its passenger locomotive stock to operate the service.

The competition was certainly fierce, and much of the pre-Group competitive fervour overlapped well into LMS/LNER days. This was responsible to a large extent for providing, right to the end of the Cheshire Lines existence, a quite rare brand of excitement, in the form of the Manchester–Liverpool speedway! You may query the word speedway, thinking perhaps that it is an over dramatisation of

Over the decades Trafford Park Depot played host to a whole family of 4-4-0s.

Above:
Great Central 4-4-0 No 1022 on the London Extension c1910. Robinson's first 4-4-0 for the company (LNER Class 'D9') is working what appears to be a local train, in the vicinity of Northwood. *LGRP, courtesy David & Charles*

the truth. But believe me it was a racing track, at least in my experience of the line in the 1940s and 50s. There was always a sense of great urgency, underlined from the moment the guard blew his whistle in the huge cavern that is Manchester Central station: the sound like the echoing pistol shot that launches an Olympic runner. The immediate whirlwind acceleration told there was not a minute to lose on very tight schedules. The seed that created an illusion of high speed as the journey developed, was planted before we even reached the platform ends. Don't misunderstand me: speed was high relative to the type of motive power and the various restrictions allied to the short distance between the two cities. Certainly travelling in one of the Cheshire Lines hourly 'expresses' gave a distinct sensation of hustle and hurry not always apparent on some of our more elite main lines. It's the sort of experience that these days I associate with the exit from that very much gloomier modern cavern called Euston, when my electric express seems to soar up Camden Bank like something rocket propelled and never appears to let up until we are slowing, relatively, for Rugby.

Something of the spirit of the working seemed to emanate from the particular type of steam power used. This for many years, almost to the end of steam working, was in the form of elderly superannuated pre-Group express 4-4-0s, mainly ex-Great Central but occasionally in latter days there were some quite notable visitors.

A most unusual manifestation of Cheshire Lines policy allowed provision for all the physical requirements of steam operation namely, coaling, watering, depot cover and simple maintenance, etc, but not of course either the motive power or staff, this being provided by the parent companies. In the main it became, by agreement, the responsibility of the Great Central/LNER, principally because of the close proximity of Gorton Works and Depot with its very comprehensive facilities for heavy repairs and general maintenance.

There were eight depots on the Cheshire Lines, which it might be useful to list: Birkenhead, Brunswick (Liverpool), Chester (Northgate), Heaton Mersey (Stockport), Northwich, Southport,

Trafford Park (Manchester), Walton on the Hill (Liverpool).

It was an unusual and indeed unique situation, just one of the many facets of railway operation in pre- and post-Grouping days that made them so endlessly fascinating. Though the Great Central/LNER provided the lion's share of motive power for operating Cheshire Lines services, and therefore were the basic users of the facilities at all eight depots, the Midland did have a sort of toehold. The reason for this was that

Below:
Great Central 4-4-0 Class 11A (LNER 'D6') No 855 c1914. Though I cannot positively identify the location I think that the train is on the Liverpool–Manchester section of the Cheshire Lines. When they were displaced from the London Extension by the 'D9s' from about 1902 onwards the '11As' became the mainstay of the more elite Cheshire Lines services for the next 30 years. The engine is seen in its original condition. *Real Photos collection*

Below right:
Great Central 4-4-0 No 875 at Trafford Park. Judging by appearances this could be shortly after rebuilding with superheater boiler and extended smokebox, this was the main basic change in the lives of the Class '11A' ('D6'). Perhaps I hardly need mention another more minor change in chimneys that so disfigured many Great Central in later years! *Real Photos*

although the Midland/LMS operated express and some local services out of Manchester Central station, it possessed no suitable depot of its own in the Manchester area to service them: Bellevue depot by virtue of its position was not a contender. Other than the latter the nearest Midland sheds on the Derby or Sheffield lines would be 40 miles away at Rowsley or Millhouses. Consequently the Midland/LMS did use the depots at Trafford Park and Heaton Mersey, but in the main for locomotives operating their own services – a sort of landlord/tenant situation, it would seem.

I have called Trafford Park and Heaton Mersey the Cheshire Lines twins because in a way they seemed to complement each other. Trafford Park was much the larger of the two and, being born in 1895, six years the younger. Both died in early 1968, very greatly mourned by local enthusiasts and probably a host of others. Both offered double-barrelled names of the kind that intrigue the visitor to the English countryside, but there similarity ended for in both function and setting they were in complete contrast. In very general terms it could be said that the depot at Trafford Park was passenger orientated while that at Heaton Mersey, with one or two notable exceptions, was mainly goods with a little local passenger work.

Trafford Park shed, though sited in what had become a rather drab industrial area, had a kind of remoteness amidst its myriad lines and sidings. The main line to Liverpool ran east–west to the south of the shed, while to the north a wide semi-circular sweep of the Bridgewater Canal completed a sort of protective enclave providing something of a barrier to approach by road. Thus cocooned it radiated a mystique heavily emphasised by the constantly unfolding romance of its locomotive complements. An approach for railwayman and enthusiast alike was provided by a footbridge across the main line and thence by a cinder track.

The name of the shed is taken from the area of which it was part. The house, park, lakes and land of Trafford Park had, like so many of the great private estates of Britain, a history reaching back to medieval times. It has been the family home of the de Traffords for little short of a thousand years (1021–1897). By the end of the 19th century it had virtually become the victim of a huge encircling movement. It lay like an innocent in the path of commercial giants of the day. For well over a century it had been bounded to the east and south by the Duke of Bridgewater's canal system. Then, with the rising tide of industrialisation, the pincers began to grip. The 19th century grew older and gradually matured, but the wine had a

tainted, smokey tang. Long dormant energy was beginning to find an outlet through the rather ponderous developments in mechanisation for both transport and industry. Business empires were in the making, though the interests of progress brought the rigours of soot and sweat for a less fortunate mass of toiling humanity.

The unfortunate de Traffords found themselves with a new railway to the south and, what in effect was the final straw, a gigantic new canal complex on the northern and eastern edges of their land. Constructed on a massive scale that doubtless was beyond the wildest imagination of the time, the Manchester Ship Canal was intended to bypass Liverpool and bring some of the world's largest cargo ships virtually to Manchester's back door. This was all very well, but in doing so they came loud and clear in the view of the de Traffords, even when they were in the hitherto seclusion of the great house. Clearly Sir Humphrey de Trafford did not take kindly to substituting distant tree-lined vistas for the masts and funnels of what must have appeared like giants stalking the end of his gardens. Obviously the hierarchy in Trafford Hall, who may

well have viewed the quiet narrow Bridgewater Canal in terms that saw small as beautiful, found no redeeming features in the latest development. There is no doubt that vastness of scale can sometimes be equated with an overbearing

ugliness. Sir Humphrey threw in the towel, gave up and sold out – and who could blame the poor fellow? Though I imagine it must have been quite a wrench after so many centuries of family history at that place.

The speculators stepped in and in due course Trafford Park gained the sort of notoriety one would expect of a large industrial complex – an area of 'dark satanic mills'. It was something of romance in reverse, where rustic farms and sylvan glades were gradually transformed and beauty became a beast of industrial progress. A green land was turned into a torn and tortured place in which man might ply his new found mechanical skills in the war against nature we call the industrial revolution.

The non-railway enthusiast might consider Trafford Park shed to be as spartan and functional of appearance as any of the other grim buildings in this scarred wasteland, though in fact it was little different from many others of its kind up and down the country. Very few were endowed with the sort of profile that inclined them towards architectural glory. But the romance and allure came not from the bricks and mortar: they provided no more than a cavernous housing for the locomotive jewels therein – be they tarnished links of dusky pearls, emeralds green or rubies red. Some were gems beyond price, especially in terms of the 1980s, but in the fullness of time they were ground to dust in the late 1950s and early 1960s, the days of our great lament.

The vintage period of the shed, for me at least, was that of the 1940s and early 1950s when it housed members of J. G. Robinson's first major passenger design for the Great Central Railway. This was a superb 4-4-0 which in its lifetime saw several rebuildings and variants and ultimately became LNER Class 'D9'. When brand new these engines were used on the recently completed 'London Extension' which, striking deep between older rivals, became a heroic contender for a long coveted crown. Now three companies competed to provide London with the most elite service to the Midlands and the northwest. Both Crewe and Derby had laid claim to this crown of pre-eminence but it never quite rested on one head. Derby had built a palace at St Pancras suitable for such a headpiece. Crewe relied on a great reputation and a huge Doric Arch. The London Extension

Above:
Trafford Park 27 August 1957 as No 41185 proceeds off depot for Manchester Central to take out the 7.30pm to Derby. The signalbox in the background protected such movement to the main line, which runs in front of the box and just below the flats to the right of the picture. The gravel path in the immediate foreground gave access to the depot from Chester Road, crossing the main line by means of a footbridge. *Raymond Keeley*

Right:
One of the elegant Fowler 2-6-4 tanks entering Manchester Central with the 8am ex-Buxton Midland on 28 February 1959. The engine, No 42370, has the Buxton 9D shed code. It will be noted in this, and also the photograph of No 46158 on the 7.5am ex-Buxton, that although only local trains the very comfortable ex-LMS corridor stock is in use. *Raymond Keeley*

Below right:
Manchester Central on 5 April 1957; Compound No 41118 recently ex-works (see also *Memories of LMS Steam*) on one of those lovely idyllic slow trains that ambled their way to Chinley. *Raymond Keeley*

ended somewhat unheroically in a large barn of a place, though a charmingly rusticated frontage made some amends. But the station never quite matched the magnificently costumed princes of the rail who rested therein, for indeed the 'D9s' were only the forerunners of a series of opulent locomotive designs to appear in that place.

Thus superceded by ever more glamorous shapes from the Robinson drawing boards at Gorton, they found rather more mundane duties. After a long life in the shadows some of the 'D9's eventually surfaced for a final fling on the Cheshire Lines racetrack. The bones may have been old and arthritic but they were to prove that life still remained. Unlike old soldiers theirs was not to fade away but to leave in a blaze of glory.

The 'D9s', so quickly overshadowed by the later 'Directors' (LNER 'D10/11'), were in some respects a 'prettier' engine. While the 'Directors' had a hefty masculinity, the 'D9s', at least in their rebuilt form, had a hefty femininity – a sort of buxom charm, if I may use the phrase. The most noticeable difference between the two types of engine to allow for such a description, is in the line of the splashers. The 'D9s' had the superb double-S familiar in some older and more splender 4-4-0s though not so common in engines of the size of a 'D9', especially after they had been reboilered.

If a 'D9' headed your train at Manchester Central then it was usually a guarantee of an exciting run to Liverpool. The timings with a stop at Warrington were tight, and this was reflected in the usually rapid acceleration out of the station. Travelling perhaps in the first compartment of the first coach, one could clearly feel the forward tug and pull from every cracking exhaust beat. The sense of animal vigour, of great limbs lunging towards the gallop was dramatically underlined and further accentuated by the curving exit from the platform ends.

Acceleration out on to the Cornbrook viaducts would be rapid and since these carried the tracks well above the rooftop level of surrounding buildings, there was a distinct sensation of 'take off'. The viaducts, still standing well into their second decade without trains, soared over an area of canal and early industry, which was in effect the eastward terminus of the Bridgewater system. Remains of a complex of wharves and basins can still be clearly seen, representing a microcosm of the early and mid-19th century industrial/transport age. When sauntering anywhere in the area one can almost smell and certainly feel the atmosphere of that time.

The great girdered structure of the viaducts dominates, carried in part on huge cylindrical columns, iron-banded and vast in girth, stretching high in giant strides across the development of an earlier age so clearly visible layer on layer, typifying the rapid mechanical/technological changes of the last 150 years – a century and a half that has seen such vast man made changes to the face of the planet.

The rapid fall to something like the surrounding ground level of what is a comparatively flat area brought ever increasing speed as the train swept across the Cornbrook Junctions; then the heat was really on.

Riding behind these somewhat elderly 4-4-0s when they were travelling fast always gave the impression of a much greater speed than was really the case, especially to an observer in the first coach. This was partially due to the see-saw motion of big driving wheels on a short wheelbase, plus the thrust and throw of inside cylinder connecting rods being confined to a narrow lateral line. Like most big inside-cylinder 4-4-0s with high pitched boilers, the wheelbase was short in comparison to the mass of the engine. This seemed to accentuate greatly the sensation of tugging and oscillation, especially as speed increased, though this only served to generate more excitement for the enthusiast.

In these days of diesel-electric traction, trains appear to glide, or so it would seem to the passenger or platform observer. Not so with steam: high speed hurry through suburban stations – and it might be at no more than 50mph – gave a quite different impression. Like the passing of some giant beast, threshing madly and breathing fire with a roar that appeared to make platform awnings shudder in protest, the very air seemed quivering and vibrant. Even the most blase was held – momentarily transfixed until the platform stones were stilled again. From the train in the lengthening distance, a furious exhaust could be heard shouting and battering at each overbridge that dared to get in its way.

The going was fairly level for a few miles until it became necessary to soar high and over the Manchester Ship Canal, achieved by a massive earthen ramp leading on to a high girder bridge. Again one had the sensation of leaving terra firma and taking flight – a feeling accentuated by miles of comparatively flat country on each side. All the time the engine angrily protested as this barrier put a brake on speed, and the headlong gallop of racer and chariot become a haltered dray horse leaning through the shafts of its ploughshare. Then suddenly, with a metalled drum roll, the line passed through the high girders with, possibly, a bird's eye view of a ship in the massive Irlam Locks. Then down the other side of the see-saw with speed gradually becoming breakneck again until it reached the 60s (though in those days the magic 'mile a minute' seemed a more hectic rate of progression than today's 100 plus in the smooth cushioned comfort of an HST). At Padgate speed would still be high and you might begin to wonder what would happen when the galloping 4-4-0 hit the junction and curving turn off for the Warrington loop. Indeed when hurtling round that curve, with a creaking and groaning from carriage framework and springs and a sensation of being pressed hard against the side of the compartment, logic suggested that the wheels were only touching the line on the outer edge of the curve! That was in the days before a different form of traction made superalignment of track and more heavily canting of curves on some main lines an absolute essential, even though it may have removed some of the 'helter skelter' fun.

The excitement was not yet over for a rapid rate of progression seemed to continue almost to the edge of the platform ramps at Warrington Central, the waiting throng passing as in a blur – were we going to stop? that was the question. Then it seemed that all anchors were dropped to claw madly at the track bed, as we achieved what was almost an emergency stop. However one should not suggest for a moment that these drivers were tear-aways: they were highly skilled specialists who had brought the operation of trains on this line to a fine art. They had exactly the 'feel' of the mighty iron steeds they were riding, and they extracted every second of rapid movement that was possible within the limits of very tight operational control of machines that, in no uncertain way, physically and visibly demonstrated, through the scale of their mechanical movement, awesome strength and power.

Elsewhere I never experienced anything quite like those sharp stops at Warrington Central. Today the closest one can get to it is the similar but much smaller scale experience on the London

Right:
'Then at the eleventh hour!' Manchester Central on 9 July 1965 as one of Fairburn's developments of the Stanier 2-6-4T No 42113, is seen on the 4.38pm stopping train to Irlam. *Gordon Coltas*

Underground when, from a distant rumble, a snaking caterpillar of vehicles hurtles from its burrow to come to a complete and abrupt stop in a slightly larger illuminated burrow. Thus the pace continued to Liverpool Central, earning that short distance between the two cities the reputation of a racetrack, and bringing exhilarating moments into the lives of some notable 4-4-0s in their old age. For them it was an 'Indian Summer' and an opportunity for rejuvenation and sparkle.

This provision of vintage passenger motive power for the Cheshire Lines main line was in itself quite unique. Other railways, as the size and scope of their locomotive fleets developed, used older express types, particularly 4-4-0s, on some of the secondary line work. However, these older engines were usually interspersed with other more modern types, especially in later years and during the Grouping period. On the Cheshire Lines the use of 4-4-0s had been almost exclusive for decades right into the late 1950s. The reason for this can in some part be found in the Great Central's locomotive policies for it was the GC – and latterly, the LNER – that provided the CLC motive power.

At the formation of the Great Central the express motive power requirements, as on so many other railways at that time, were vested in the 4-4-0. There had been a history of development of the type on the Manchester Sheffield and Lincolnshire Railway. Then, in 1897, Harry Pollitt brought out a 4-4-0 for the newly built London Extension, the opening of which and the new found prestige, caused the name of the company to change. Its rather mundane title was transformed into one that still lives in enthusiasts' memories. A simple title, Great Central, but invested with an aura of glamour, which was soon to be matched by its splendid locomotives. The development of the 4-4-0 continued under John G. Robinson after his appointment to the position of Locomotive Engineer of the new company in 1900. His first express locomotive design for the London Extension proved to be a slightly inflated version of the last Pollit design, an engine that, in its superb reboilered style, became familiar to my generation of enthusiasts as LNER Class 'D9'. But Robinson was soon on his way to more grandiose concepts as his attention, spurred no doubt by the commercial ambitions of the dynamic Sam Fay, turned to greater things in the form of delectable Atlantics and mighty 4-6-0s – images in steam and steel that had the imprint of the great artist.

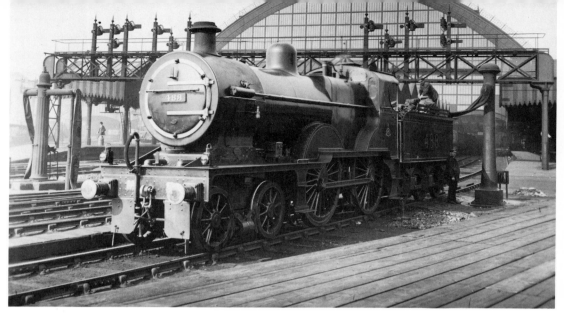

**This most interesting photograph shows
Manchester Central at a much earlier time. Dated
probably between 1912 and 1914, the engine is
Johnson 4-4-0 No 488 of 1896 but is shown in the
rebuilt form – superheater, raised running plate,
modified splashers etc – as introduced by Fowler
in 1912. The gentleman on the far platform is
clearly dressed in the late Edwardian style. The
signal gantry is of great interest, pre-Acfield and
probably dating from the early days of the
station's life. Both driver and fireman are looking
very suspiciously at the photographer, the
excellence of whose work is such that the shed
code on the smokebox (1), which is Derby, can
easily be identified on the print.** *Ian Allan
Library*

Surprisingly, one of his most breathtaking designs was not one of these locomotives but stemmed from a reversion to
an earlier and certainly less grandiose
style. It was a 4-4-0 that was undoubtedly
his masterpiece – the magnificent 'Director'
class (LNER 'D11'). These engines became
and remain, for a generation of enthusiasts, a legend and an enigma – legendary
for their great size for an inside-cylinderd
4-4-0 and for their achievements. An
enigma, tantalisingly, for what we are
convinced they might have achieved
under even more arduous working condi-

tions than existed on the Great Central
main line. Sadly the chance of a sort of
ultimate testing of power output and
capacity never came their way. It remained
for their rivals on that other great main
line to find that sort of opportunity – the
gritty but spendid 'George V' 4-4-0s of
Bowen Cooke which, in their heyday,
were hauling prodigious loads between
Euston and Carlisle, and in the process
earning their own very special legend.

Thus the potential of the 'Directors' in
absolute terms, with their lightly loaded
trains on the Great Central main line,
must remain unknown. They did, however, during the LNER period, give some
of the larger rivals that worked with them
a run for their money. They held their
own almost to the exclusion of Robinson's
own magnificent 4-6-0s, and in latter days
even Gresley's splendid 'Sandringham'
class 4-6-0s found the challenge of the
'Directors' did not allow the easy ascen-
dancy one might have expected for a
modern passenger 4-6-0.

So it came about that over the earlier
decades of this century the Cheshire Lines
played host to a whole family of 4-4-0s
from the one stable. In each case it was a
bit like racehorses being put out to grass
because these engines found duty on the

Cheshire Lines mainly as a result of being displaced elsewhere. It seemed a clear cut parent company policy (both Great Central and LNER in turn) to relegate what they considered the 'ancients' of their passenger locomotive stock to secondary duties or the Cheshire Lines. Indeed, this was perpetuated for at least the first 10 years of British Railways – truly, a most agreeable policy for the resident enthusiasts!

The most extreme and perhaps most notable example of this policy was seen when some of the mighty 'Directors' were shedded at Trafford Park. But the Cheshire Lines stint did not prove to be a finale for these 'English' members of the Class 'D11'. Early in 1958, 10 of the 11 engines of the class (including the half dozen which had been rusting away in the open at Trafford Park but excepting No 62663 at Staveley) were transferred to Sheffield (Darnall) for a final – if brief – moment of glory. (This episode is described in *Memories of LNER Steam.*) Most certainly the light and fire of these splendid engines departed this world with an enviable fanfare and flourish and it is entirely appropriate that *Butler Henderson* should continue to steam on representing the Great Central at its best.

In the last decade or so of steam the Great Central 4-4-0s worked the service almost by themselves, with but spasmodic assistance. Some of this help was provided by very distinguished visitors – but more of that anon. Then, at the eleventh hour, somewhere in the higher echelons of motive power organisation, a light appeared to dawn. Surely this was a service ideal for operation by modern passenger tank engines. Something like the Stanier 2-6-4s, or their derivatives, would give all the power and flexibility required. The lessons in this sort of operating economy had been learned half a century before on the 'Brighton' and on the London Tilbury and Southend. However, it seemed it was never too late to learn, but by the time the 2-6-4Ts were proving their undoubted capability and operational economy the DMUs were on the scene. For the enthusiasts it was marvellous while it lasted; indeed none of us would have complained if the 'D9s', 'Directors', etc had gone on for another couple of decades.

'What about those etceteras' you might say! These were the distinguished visitors mentioned earlier – and distinguished indeed they were.

It happened 'out of the blue' or at least 'out of the green of East Anglia' and was quite unexpected, yet in a way in keeping with the policy of using four-coupled motive power on the longer Cheshire Lines passenger services. The enthusiast might well have rubbed his eyes in disbelief when in late 1949 a Great Eastern 'Claud Hamilton' (LNER Class 'D16') 4-4-0 turned up at Trafford Park, followed about six months later by a further seven of the class. All except one of these were shedded at Trafford Park and rarely could the great arched roof at Manchester Central have given cover to more distinguished visitors. Indeed in ornamentation and beauty of line they were only seriously rivalled by the resident Midland Compounds.

It seemed a curious move for a locomotive type rarely seen outside the counties and environs of its native East Anglia and in some respects, out of step with a long tradition at Trafford Park. One could speculate and wonder why, if it was essential to augment the ageing 'D9s' and handful of 'D11s' on the Cheshire Lines, the modern 2-6-4T idea did not catch on even earlier. Apart from the latter method of resolving the problem, one wonders at the possibility of bringing a few of the Scotish 'Directors' south: at least tradition and a familiarity of handling would have been maintained. Perhaps there were administrative problems concerned with such a move, though one imagines that also applied to the 'D16s'. There may also have been a problem of spares with the 'D16s', since some of the engines spent lengthy periods on shed awaiting maintenance – with Stratford Works at the other end of the country it may have been a case of 'out of sight, out of mind', whereas the proximity of Gorton Works would have led to fewer problems with the ex-Great Central classes. However the very welcome visit of the 'Clauds' lasted for all too short a time; by mid-1952 they had returned east. If this brief stay may be considered ill-judged, it should not therefore be seen as reflecting any criticism of the engines, since when given the opportunity they apparently performed quite well. Indeed it is hard to imagine these engines being anything other than successful wherever they ran, especially since their legendary power and performance on the Great Eastern main line is part of the saga of the British steam locomotive's achievements. They join the ranks of those other 4-4-0s – the 'Directors', 'George Vs', Midland Compounds and, more recently, the Maunsells 'Schools' class – which in their time offered the most severe competition to modern 4-6-0s!

If this brief interlude of Great Eastern promise was something of a puzzle, it was certainly an unexpected bonus for the enthusiasts. Of course the move may have had something to do with the fact that it was still early days on the recently nationalised railways; time of arbitary regional demarcations that may have created some uncertainties. Doubtless such could have caused some hesitation, even confusion, in terms of locomotive policy and planning, especially in secondary areas where an overlapping of regional interests may have caused conflicting views on the use of motive power. It was not so much a problem on the main lines – on both East and West Coast main lines of the ex-LMS/LNER a tradition and style of modern steam motive power continued with scarcely a ripple during the decade or so of change from the end of World War 2 into the early years of British Rail.

Thus the enigma, for that is how I see it, of the great trek to the northwest of the 'D16s', remains. But then it is not the first time in the history of steam in Britain that the unexpected has happened. It would certainly be the poorer were it not endowed with such riches!

If the Great Central/LNER provided the motive power for most Cheshire Lines services operated by Trafford Park, the shed, as mentioned earlier, also provided a home for Midland/LMS motive power used on the main line to Derby and some branch line services. Thus Midland 4-4-0s, and in particular the Compounds, joined the ranks of other notables of that wheel arrangement on the shed. In the middle and late 1950s the Compounds were occasionally seen on the Liverpool expresses, but primarily were used on the Derby main line. They were also the backbone at that time of that excellent but meandering branch that crossed the V of the Derby–Manchester and Derby–Sheffield lines between Chinley South Junction and Dore, now of course the 'main' line twixt Manchester and Sheffield. (My article 'Hope Valley Line' in *Railway World Annual 1980* covers this.)

There is more than a hint in the previous paragraph to another aspect of the many sided locomotive personality presented by Trafford Park – the Midland main line to London St Pancras.

When, just over 100 years ago, the Midland finally made it into the new and magnificent Manchester Central station, it was considered that it had a terminus in the Cottonopolis worthy of its trains and engines. It was arranged that stabling for its locomotives would be provided by the Cheshire Lines at Trafford Park, shared of course with the main provider of Cheshire Lines motive power, the Great Central/LNER. In retospect I always think it surprising that the Midland did not go for a depot of their own suitable for the new main line, especially as there was no shortage of sites at the turn of the century. It does seem out of character with their singleminded determination to get on their own tracks – well almost! – into the centre of Manchester. Certainly a depot of their own would have been in keeping with the constant search for prestige and area autonomy which, I believe, had become a sort of psychological necessity for a railway sandwiched between the East and West Coast entrepreneural giants.

However it was not to be and so started a long saga of Midland, LMS and finally British Rail main line locomotive presence at Trafford Park. From the elegance of the Compounds to the look of hunched tearaway competence presented by the 'Britannias' and, in between most of the LMS 'big guns' short of the Stanier Pacifics, appeared 'Scots', 'Jubilees', Class '5s' etc. I suppose the schoolboy observers of the 1930s, of which I was one, never in their widest dreams expected to see regular Pacific workings on that particular Midland main line. But then we never bargained for quite the versatility the 'Brits' brought to that particular chassis.

With thoughts of those exciting locomotives in mind the narrative moves south to a well watered valley that could, one imagines, in another age have moved the poet to verse or a budding Constable to brush and easel. The railway brought an animal vigour and a certain elegance, removed by a more utilitarian age. While nature has struggled, hardly more than a vestige of beauty now remains.

Below:
Almost half a century on from the previous photograph (though I was still photographing one or two of those Fowler rebuilds in the late 1950s – see *Memories of LMS Steam!*) the date now being 6 October 1961, Ivatt 2-6-0 No 43037 awaits the 'right away' with the 4.10pm to Chinley. The shed code on the smokebox (41C) denotes Millhouses. *Raymond Keeley*

3 Steam Shed Magic

. . . straight lines and roundhouses

It is almost impossible now, after more than a century and a half of mechanical and technical progress, to imagine the enormous scale of the problems facing the early railway engineers. They were, after all, probing ahead into a relatively unexplored world of new and untried technology that involved, quite apart from building and developing the steam locomotive, almost every other area of engineering and building construction.

Among the many problems facing them, probably from the earliest time a steam locomotive moved on its own railway track, was the requirement that an engine had to be able to turn back to front from its own fixed directional position on that track. The solution now seems simple enough in restrospect, but obvious and simple solutions to problems are usually only seen that way with hindsight! However, those early pioneers, being men of skill and ingenuity, found an answer which meant, as time progressed, being able to turn longer and heavier units with precision and perfect balance.

In due course this requirement for turning plus the need for shelter would ultimately produce the roundhouse and the straight line shed. Both were viable but completely contrasting methods of locomotive housing, giving the option of a turntable incorporated in the main shed building or in a separate area of the shed yards.

Clearly as railway systems developed during the 19th century many things influenced depot layout. Most important was size because as services – and, therefore, locomotive complements – expanded,

so too would the needs of the depot. Then district environment and therefore the amount of space available at a chosen place had to be taken into consideration: which leads to the one factor that could not be ignored or changed – geographical setting. The lie of the land, curve in a river, etc (see Chapter 2) were vital factors that had great bearing on the whole layout of the various buildings and servicing units that comprised a depot.

Although one might expect the above considerations to play an important part in deciding whether to build a roundhouse or straight line shed, it did seem that some pre-Group companies had a clear policy on the method to be used, when other considerations made both possible. Certainly the roundhouse did predominate on the old North Eastern Railway and obviously found favour on the Midland, though I believe it would be true to say that throughout the country the roundhouse type was greatly outnumbered by the straight line variety.

To a degree the advantages of each tended to cancel each other out, though in my view the roundhouse still had the edge, as I will explain later. Probably when it came down to basics it was very much a matter of economics. Even in an age when the phrase 'cash flow problems' did not have the wide publicity and emphasis of our present age, these problems were probably still very apparent to those directly involved in trying to achieve the best return for the shareholders.

Doubtless land value and rateable values also had a great influence. So it is understandable that a company like the old North Eastern, operating in areas where such costs were likely to be lower than in and around the big conurbations, could and did favour the roundhouse. In contrast the London & North Western seemed to prefer the very compact straight line type, a choice which perhaps fitted that company's reputation for the spartan approach, for there is little evidence to suggest it ever ventured far from the bare minimum of structures and motive power to operate services. Great economy in the use of resources was underlined by the lack of ostentation or ornament at places like Euston or New Street Birmingham, and in locomotives that the great overlord at Crewe, in the company's halcyon days, decreed should be in any colour so long as it was black! For all that the London & North Western was a great railway managed with the sort of business efficiency that would raise approving eyebrows in the late 20th century.

'. . . the requirement that an engine had to be able to turn back to front from its own fixed directional position on that track!'

Below:
All roads lead to – well, in this case to Camden's famous turntable in July 1949. It seems appropriate that the table should be occupied by the doyen of LMS passenger locomotives, particularly as No 46256 is named *Sir William A Stanier F.R.S.* *Stewart Blencowe collection*

In recollection and consideration of sheds/depots one thing emerges quite clearly, that no two of them, be they roundhouses or straight line buildings, ever seemed to have a common disposition of buildings. I cannot imagine any enthusiast mistaking the identity of the particular shed he happened to be in. The resultant unique nature of a depot did much to create 'character'.

Many other different factors contributed to the character of a depot. The shape or form of the main buildings gave an initial identity, even though in general they were plain brick structures mostly devoid of any ornamentation and, in a sense, inert. Obviously the locomotive complement played a large part and could contribute something to the romance and atmosphere of certain notable places. Just a whiff of 'Kings' and 'Castles' at Old Oak Common and one could almost sense the tang of sea air and the green and ancient West Country. Camden – just say the word and its overtones ripple to the sound of a Pacific blasting over the top of that fearsome two-mile incline from Euston.

In the final analysis it is district's environment and the nature of the locomotive complement plus that most important additional ingredient – the human viewpoint – which produced the character of a depot. Since the whole intellect – the psyche of each enthusiast who was captured by the atmosphere

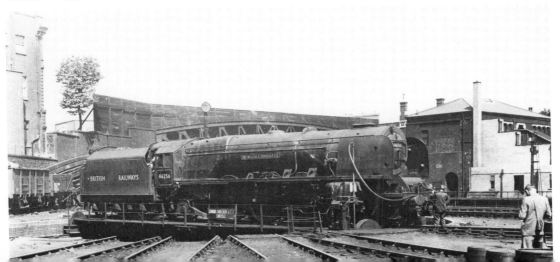

inside a steam shed – was unique to that person, then each person in his own way helped to create the character. When the names of some of these places were spoken – Kingmoor, Nine Elms, Dairycoates etc – one sensed, momentarily, an almost hushed tone, such was their power to bewitch. Each was a temptress beckoning and we, poor mortals, had little power to resist. We had our favourite and familiar depots and, for that matter, railway companies, and it is from the distilling of that unearthly chemistry within our being, influenced by circumstance, opportunity and emotion, that each hallowed locomotive dwelling assumes its special cloak of character and personality.

It seems incredible that even at the end of steam in Britain, the majority of steam depots were a legacy of companies which had gone out of existence almost half a century before; a tribute indeed to the soundness of the planning and building techniques of those earlier days. For those of us alive during the three or four decades after the Grouping, it was a legacy beyond price.

I mentioned earlier that the advantages and disadvantages of the two different types of layout within the running shed were inclined to cancel each other out. The roundhouse, though taking up probably well in excess of 100% more room per square yard of locomotive space, had the advantage of much more light and working

Below:
The Gorton turntable on 9 March 1958. No 63848 of Class '04/7' is one of many variations tried on that great locomotive family, the Robinson 2-8-0s. This one is basically as originally built but with the Belpaire boiler replaced by a GNR/LNER 02 type. *Raymond Keeley*

Below right:
Carnforth on 27 March 1982 where S&D 2-8-0 No 13809 is executing an about turn after completing a leg of the 'Cumbrian Mountain Pullman'. I wonder how many visitors to the steam centre pause to admire the very distinctive Furness signalbox seen in the background? *Raymond Keeley*

area around each locomotive and, if required, the latter could be left in situ almost indefinitely. The generous allowance of space in a roundhouse, which of course increased proportionately to the distance each radial line extended from the centre point, was accentuated by the need for each to house its own turntable.

In the straight line shed one might say that a maximum of locomotive space was housed in an absolute minimum area. Conditions in the average shed of this type were certainly uncomfortable and to some unfortunate people they would be claustrophobic to say the least. Lighting was minimal: even in the days of electricity the interior seemed a place of perpetual twilight. One can only imagine what it might have been like in the days when oil lamps would be the only means of illumination, themselves adding to an atmosphere already heavy laden with a sulphuric gloom. Engines seemed bigger than ever, almost menacingly so as they crouched over the scuttering mortals who attended them. But it was a marvellously supercharged atmosphere, at least for the enthusiast who could afford to remain somewhat detached from the discomforts. It heavily underlined various emotional responses: the lift of spirit when the cabside number appearing out of the smokey fog is the 'Hall', 'Shire', 'King Arthur' so long awaited; being close enough to touch great driving wheels – to sense the intricacy, the massive scale of link motion and eccentrics; the atmosphere itself, the whole place pungent with the smell of warm coal smoke, dank steam and a pervading aroma of oily working parts. Whether the poor devil who had to work in such cramped conditions saw it that way is another matter. Certainly the working space for engines being cleaned, undergoing light repairs or being prepared for work, required at times the contortions of an acrobat. Doubtless the valiant volunteers of today would say amen to that.

A major problem in a straight line shed would be that of moving and repositioning. Getting engines on and off shed in the right order, moving engines requiring minor attention out of the way of

those fit for duty, to mention but two of the problems, must at times have been a nightmare – especially at a large shed catering for many different sorts of duty. There were doubtless occasions when a shedmaster would feel like a general manouvring an armoured division, or as if he was involved in some sort of devilish fantasy of chessboard moves, with chaos as the result of the wrong permutations. Even if you got it right it could be an involved time consuming operating.

The enthusiast however, not involved with the cost/efficiency aspects of the previous paragraphs, could afford to take a different view of the two basic layouts, being influenced perhaps more by feelings than the practical or economic problems they posed. I believe that both forms of layout touched different chords in our emotional make up which broadly speaking, can be summed up thus: one appealed to a more extrovert side of our nature the other was more introvert in its attraction.

I have already hinted at the more introvert aspects of the straight line shed

'The roundhouse, though taking up probably well in excess of 100% more room of locomotive space, had the advantage of much more light and working area around each locomotive'

Above:
It required a little detective work to establish the whereabouts and date of this photograph. The presence of an L&Y 2-4-2T among strange bedfellows provided the first clue for, on 28 September 1957, No 50781 in company with GWR 'Dukedog' No 9021 ran a special for the Talyllyn Railway Preservation Society from Shrewsbury to Towyn. Unfortunately the tank suffered piston packing gland problems and was replaced by a BR Standard 2-6-0 for the return journey. Repairs were effected to No 50781 at Machynlleth and the 2-4-2 then travelled back to Shrewsbury on 3 October from where it, presumably, made its way to the home shed of Southport. The roundhouse is identified as Shrewsbury (ex-GWR roundhouse) the date being on or about 3 October 1957. *Stewart Blencowe collection*

where what could be described as an atmosphere of concealment existed, and may well have appealed to a deeper subconscious part of our being. Certainly if

Swindon running shed on 21 June 1955, showing 0-4-2T No 1446; 0-6-0 pannier tank No 3737; and 2-6-2T No 5555. *Alan Blencowe*

you were in a hurry to get down as many numbers as possible in a quick visit up and down the rows, then the straight line shed had some advantages. The problem was that you never had much more than a glimpse above your head of a number that was quite likely to be indistinct and grimy, and a towering bulk of steel and metalwork lost into the gloom. Such a view, especially of the larger express and freight engines, was never less than impressive, but there was never sufficient space to let the eyes caress every detail of what might be a quite delectable shape. It was more a case of feeling the 'presence', of being almost engulfed by the suppressed power that surrounded on all sides. Numbers were hurriedly noted down and, if you were lucky, some might prove to be the hoped for 'cops' and provide more underlining in the home based records. In such a situation it could hardly be

more than that, a sheer statistical filling in of the gaps – the unexplainable personal satisfaction of recording something already known to exist, though of course some of the information did pertain to the interest arising out of the inter-depot movement of power units.

With a roundhouse it was quite different because each locomotive could, usually, be clearly viewed and from a variety of angles. I do not believe there can be a more endearing sight in the locomotive world than a semicircular ring of smoke-box doors nodding, metaphorically speaking, towards each other, gathered, tribal fashion, in an almost human conversational group. Such delightful and changing tableux can be seen to perfection as part of the scene at the admirable National Railway Museum.

It would seem that from the earliest civilised times – since man conceived the wheel, perhaps – that he has been bemused and fascinated by the designs arising from the use of geometric patterns. Indeed the perfect symmetry and balance that can result from the use of circular forms allied to the angular, and worked out in stone, brick, iron and timber, or, in our own times, in steel and concrete, is a major source of man's aesthetic pleasures.

Thus the roundhouse is a simple yet superb example of a basic geometric form allied to movement that fits the inate sense of order that we feel should be manifest in all our material creations. With lines radiating from a central hub it becomes the perfect fusing of the straight with the circular. The locomotive itself makes a further addition to the pattern, for is it not so that the kaleidascope of rotary, horizontal and perpendicular motion in the driving wheels, coupling/connecting rods of a great express steam locomotive is one of its most beguiling features?

Within the roundhouse engines stand in orderly array, then each in its turn moves slowly forward to swing lazily on the turntable, obeying within that movement and its own a sort of central harmonious perfection. At York, in the present, and many other places in the past, enthusiasts would stand transfixed as they watched this simple but wonderful movement.

Long ago the railway photographer discovered the roundhouse with its endless possibilities for composition and dramatic effect. Indeed some of the most eloquent and evocative photographs of the steam engine at rest are those showing them pointing towards the central turntable. Infinite were the light and shade effects possible, these being sometimes caught, by the more imaginative person with a camera, in a way that placed the resultant print in the realms of the greatest artistry.

The old North Eastern Railway, being somewhat partial to the roundhouse method, could claim some magnificent examples of the genre. One of my favourites, doubtless influenced by the locomotive complements on the few occasions I toured the depot, was Neville Hill (Leeds). During the last two or three decades of its life as a steam depot it successively housed members from some of the most distinguished locomotives families, both ex-

Below:
Carlisle Canal on 19 May 1958: locomotives on show are Gresley 0-6-2T Class 'N2' No 69564, 0-6-0 Class 'J39' No 64888 and ex-North British Holmes 0-6-0 (LNER Class 'J35') No 64499.
Alan Blencowe

North Eastern and LNER vintage. Apart from the Raven Pacifics, examples of most latter day North Eastern passenger engines lasted well into the 1940s and 50s and inevitably found their way onto the Neville Hill turntables – everything from the linear elegance of the Raven Class 'Z' Atlantics (LNER 'C7') to the classic simplicity of that handsome and surprisingly modern looking mixed traffic 4-6-0 from the Raven drawing boards the North Eastern Class 'S3' (LNER 'B16'). In the last days of steam those two Gresley beauties, the Class 'D49' 4-4-0 and the 'A3' Pacifics, joined the galaxy who seemed to bow in homage to each other across those light airy spaces.

I made a few trips to Neville Hill during the war period, but one in particular on 17 March 1945 (I also did Holbeck on that same afternoon) is particularly well remembered, and for several reasons. The holocaust in Europe was reaching its final crescendo. Rumour also had it that I and several colleagues were about to be posted overseas, possibly to the Far East where, since we then knew nothing of the atom bombing that was imminent, the vicious war in that area might continue for some time. However, taking a cue from a historical 'great' – after all Drake paused to play bowls while the Armada hovered – I, from position of insignificance, could pause briefly to view the few sculptures in steel on offer at Neville Hill and reflect on their attributes.

Of particular interest to me were the examples of Classes 'D20', 'D21', 'D49' and 'C7' that were on view. They were, of course, in the company of many other notables (too numerous to mention here) which perhaps did not occupy such a distinguished, even exotic, plane of eminence as those mentioned above. Engines on show of the four types mentioned were: 'D20' – Nos 476, 1236 (Starbeck), 2018; 'D21' – 1242, 1243; 'D49' – 297 *The Cottesmore,* 357 *The Fernie,* 365 *The Morpeth* (N.H.), 366 *The Oakley* (N.H.),

368 *The Puckeridge,* 376 *The Staintondale* (N.H.); 'C7' – 2204 (York), 2206 (York).

Incidentally, No 365 *The Morpeth* was the one 'D49' to suffer the rather dismal rebuilding by Edward Thompson which, basically, concerned replacing the rotary cam operated three cylinders of the original with a more conventional two (inside) cylinder layout more popular several decades earlier. It seemed and probably was a retrograde step. Certainly in terms of appearance the engine assumed a sort of split personality, the modern boiler and cab being allied to lower regions that had returned to the fashioned of an earlier age. The rebuild was not a success and appeared to be quietly swept under one of those carpets that are reserved for such occasions!

Each of the three types of 4-4-0 on display was particularly notable in one way or another.

The 'D20' (NE Class 'R'), Wilson Worsdell's penultimate design of 4-4-0, was really his chef-d'oeuvre, and rated very high among the many fine designs of 4-4-0 produced by the pre-Group companies during that full flowering of the type in the late Victorian/early Edwardian period. Indeed, while designers often tried to go on to bigger and more powerful locomotives, it was, so often, the intermediate product of their imagination that achieved the greatest success or is most fondly remembered. One thinks of the McIntosh 'Dunalastairs', Holden's 'Claud Hamiltons', Robinson's 'Directors', the legendary 'George Vs' of Bowen Cooke. From each of those success stories their designers launched themselves into bigger and, as they probably hoped, even greater projects. Though these were to reach varying degrees of success in no case did they quite find that level of achievement their smaller brethren are now renowned for.

Wilson Worsdell was apparently no exception for clearly he tried to go one better than the Class 'R' in his massive

'R1s' (LNER 'D21'). But the result, though visually quite breathtaking, did not, it would seem, come anywhere near the high standards of performance set by the 'Rs'. Certainly the 'D21s' were impressive; in size they ranked among the very largest pre-Group inside cylinder 4-4-0s ever built in Britain, and from the viewpoint of vehicle mass roughly equalled the 'D49s'. But the 'D21s', like certain other locomotive 'ultimates in size' of the later Edwardian period, could perhaps be likened to a theme that had run out of steam – forgive the pun! By arrival of the 'D49' design in the mid-1920s new themes were in the making (so many of which seem to have sprung from the inspiration of that great man of the Western, G. J. Churchward) and the gradually emerging and developing ideas that reached out for greater thermal efficiency and economy were becoming apparent in the shape of a newer breed of locomotives which seemed to be looking into the future.

As I said, each of the three designs of 4-4-0 on that afternoon at Neville Hill seemed to reflect something. It goes almost without saying that they reflected the good taste and feeling for fine proportions that became and remained a distinctive feature of their designers artistry. From each of the radiating positions their beauty of line seemed to grow and blossom in the sunlight and shadow.

The 'D20' represented a full flowering of ideas developed over the previous two or three decades. The 'D21', a magnificent specimen, was perhaps a little over ripe but, like a lovely full blown rose, still arresting in shape. The 'D49' was an almost casually flung down seed that, despite the sower whose mind quite likely was occupied with producing other more exotic flowers, insisted on producing a bloom that would continue to turn admiring heads.

Thus it was possible from one viewpoint, in Neville Hill's most aesthetically satisfactory roundtable arrangement of

locomotives, to see an almost full arc of 4-4-0 locomotive development, and added to the distinguished company were the two 'C7s' and a 'C6' (NE Class 'V') And what is in a number with a prefix letter? Well, in the case of the 'C7s' (NE Class 'Z') it gives identity to a breed which, had we managed to save just one, could have been holding the crowds enthralled on the West to North or the Long Drag. Of the four types of Atlantic taken over by the LNER, the North Eastern variety designed by Sir Vincent Raven certainly had the edge in the good looks stakes. The linear spread of the 'Zs' was partly accounted for by the fact that the connecting rods from each of the three cylinders drove on to the front coupled axle which necessitated moving the leading bogie forward 18 inches compared to the 'Vs'. This also resulted in an increase in the length of the smokebox and gave them an almost Regency style of graceful flowing ornamentation and a great dignity of bearing.

It seemed fitting that such a gathering of locomotive 'stars' should be able to disport themselves across so fine a stage, with the occasional opportunity to move forward and give a solo turn.

Straight lines or roundhouses, it is entirely fitting that these, the living quarters of a steam locomotive, should produce a character and personality reflecting that of its main resident. Certainly no other structures man has created ever contained so much, and so vivid a manifestation of a form of life that so successfully transcends its inert materiality.

'In a straight line shed one might say that a maximum of locomotive space was housed in an absolute minimum area!'

Below:
Sunderland, 21 May 1958 showing the two small straight sheds to the west of the roundhouse. The dark interior might beckon the enthusiast, but . . . ! The 4-6-2Ts on the left are Class 'A8' Nos 69883 and 69853. *Raymond Keeley*

Above:
Bletchley Shed, 1938. Just occasionally there may be a spot in a straight line shed sufficiently uncluttered to allow a reasonable threequarter view of a locomotive – then of course the roof supports have to intervene! However despite the obstruction – which I think adds something to the atmosphere anyway – this splendid time exposure is full of interest. The NWR engine, 'Prince of Wales' class 4-6-0 No 25845, is one of the few that were modified with an outside Walschaerts valve gear which operated, via rocking levers, the inside piston valves. The somewhat ghostly figures (time exposure doesn't favour movement!) around the boiler appear to be cleaners hard at work.
Stewart Blencowe collection

Above:
Three Bridges, on 23 June 1959, with Drummond 0-4-4T Class 'M7' No 30056 and Billington 2-6-0 Class 'K' No 32348. The single lightbulb hovering over the dome of the 'M7' will be noted.
Raymond Keeley

Below:
Inside Edge Hill shed c1932, with LMS Compound No 1111 similarly obstructed as the 'Prince' in the previous photograph. But it does show that even in the most difficult circumstances an interesting picture can sometimes be the result.
Gordon Coltas

Straight lines in the shed yards could at times offer the most beguiling studies.

Above:
Tonbridge shed on 29 August 1958.
As late in the days of steam as 1958 it was possible to get such a vintage line up – and it wasn't uncommon. All the engines in the foreground are Wainwright designs for the old South Eastern & Chatham Railway. They are, left to right, Class 'L' 4-4-0 No 31768 – built 1914, it was Wainwright's last class of 4-4-0 for that railway; a Class 'H' 0-4-4T (the class was built between 1904 and 1915); and Class C 0-6-0 No 31272 – the class was built 1900–08). Such longevity surely says a great deal for soundness of design and construction! *Raymond Keeley*

Below:
Newton Abbot shed on 2 June 1955 showing locomotive in the yards during the ASLEF strike of that year. In the foreground are Nos 6814 *Enborne Grange*, 6820 *Kingstone Grange* and No 5079 *Lysander. Alan Blencowe*

Above:
Mexborough shed on 10 May 1959 showing the versatile Robinson 2-8-0s. The one on the right, No 63758, has the 02 type boiler, while the other two, Nos 63658 and 63599, are – except for small detail – to the original design. *Raymond Keeley*

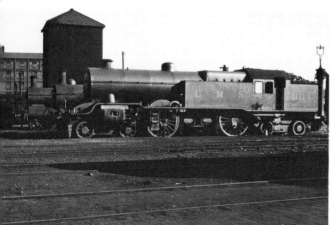

Above:
Thornton Junction on 23 August 1955 with North British 'Scott' (LNER Class 'D30') No 62419 *Meg Dods,* a Class 'J35' 0-6-0 to the left and Class 'J38' 0-6-0 No 65901 to the right. *Alan Blencowe*

Left:
Yarmouth shed in 1931. The low angle shot makes an impressive view of Class 'D16/2' No 8800, with another 'Claud' to the rear. *Gordon Coltas*

Below left:
Newton Heath in 1931. A most unusual photograph of one of my favourite L&Y locomotive types. There were precious few 'Baltic' 4-6-4Ts in Britain with four out of the five types ending up in LMS livery. The L&Y engines designed by Hughes were only 10 in total and, though successful, eventually suffered from being only a small class, especially in the standardisation programmes on the LMS that gathered momentum under Stanier. I see it as one of those interesting 'what might have beens' of history – had Hughes been younger when he became CME of the newly formed LMS, especially in the light of that company's requirement for large tank engines in the next couple of decades. No 11114 is obviously having attention to the centre pair of driving wheels, the absence of which seems to emphasise further the size and length of these great engines. *Gordon Coltas*

Above:
Fratton, 23 June 1959 with the roundhouse in the background. Billington 0-6-2T Class 'E4' No 32479 completely dwarfs the little Stroudley 'Terrier' No 32678. Class 'U' No 31804 is one of the 2-6-0s rebuilt from the 'River' class 2-6-4s after the latter had fallen into disrepute following the derailment at Sevenoaks in 1927. *Raymond Keeley*

Below:
New England, 20 July 1963 showing Class '9F' 2-10-0 No 92179; 'B1' No 61097; 'V2' No 60841, and 'Jubilee' No 45700 *Amethyst*. The latter had been renamed from *Britannia* on introduction of the 'Britannia' Pacifics. The new name was in recognition of the Royal Navy frigate *Amethyst* which escaped from Chinese hands through gunfire on the Yangste River in 1949.
Alan Blencowe

Above:
A corner of Stratford shed yards in 1932. Both
engines appear to be ex-works Class 'D13' No
8020 was a rebuild from a 2-4-0 to 4-4-0 largely
influenced by the huge success of the later 'Claud
Hamilton' 4-4-0s. Behind is Class 'F3' 2-4-2T No
8044, a Holden design built in 1902. *Gordon
Coltas*

The 'light airy spaces' of Neville Hill. The
following seven photographs have virtually a
generation between them. Two of them date from
around 1930 by a photographer unknown to me
but to whom we are indebted. We are equally
indebted to Alan Blencowe for the remaining five,
coming from the last years of steam at the depot.

Bottom left:
This and the following photograph are of great
interest showing examples of that very rare breed
in British locomotive building, the 4-4-4T. Raven
built 45 of these, very large for a four-coupled
design. No 1520 was built in 1920, then rebuilt as
a 4-6-2T in 1935 becoming LNER Class 'A8'.
Raymond Keeley collection

Below:
Neville Hill c1930 showing Class 'H1' No 1518
which was built in 1920 and rebuilt as a 4-6-2T in
1933. *Raymond Keeley collection*

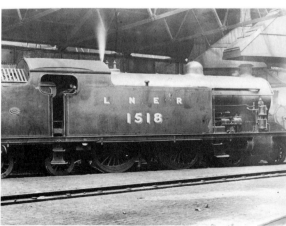

Above:
Class 'A1' No 60140 *Balmoral* (shedcode 50A York) seen at Neville Hill on 10 August 1963. *Alan Blencowe*

Below:
Class 'V2' No 60929 (shedcode 50A York) seen at Neville Hill on 10 August 1963. *Alan Blencowe*

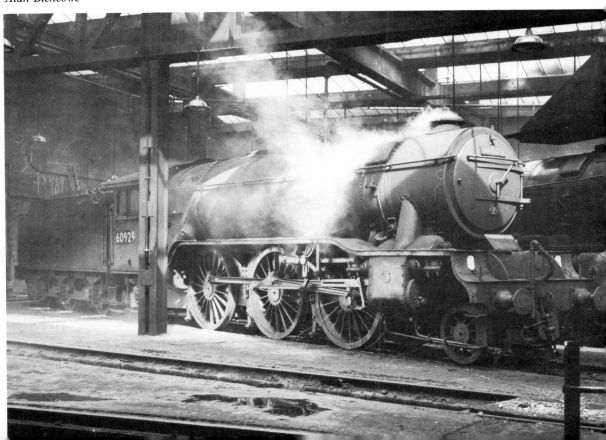

Above:
Another view of Neville Hill on 10 August 1963 showing Class 'Q6' No 63424 (shedcode 55H Neville Hill) and Stanier '3MT' 2-6-2T No 40148. *Alan Blencowe*

Peregrine **at Neville Hill with a youthful Stewart Blencowe in the left foreground.** *Alan Blencowe*

Below:
The other side of 'A1' No 60146. *Alan Blencowe*

Below:
Same place, same date – Class 'A1' No 60146

Quite apart from locomotive groups, the shed yard was the traditional place to get good side/front or threequarter 'portrait' views of a locomotive and, since the background to the sitter offered infinite variation, the permutations seemed endless. The following selection of prints serves to underline the point.

Top right:
New England, 20 July 1963, Class 'A4' No 60032 *Gannet*. Even though the appearance is somewhat tarnished and even slightly battered here and there, *Gannet* was every inch a thoroughbred. The nobility of line positively leaps out of the picture frame. At this time the engine had only a little life remaining before it was scrapped in October 1963. *Alan Blencowe*

Below:
Since I have included photographs of the North Eastern 4-4-4Ts it seemed appropriate to include the other notable design of large tank locomotive built to that wheel arrangement in Britain. The symmetrical layout of this wheel arrangement made for a particularly elegant design in the case of the Metropolitan engines. The pity is they were so few in number, but at least they did not suffer the fate of being 'improved' by rebuilding. No 107 is seen standing against the coaling stage at Neasden: what seem to be wickerwork coal tubs are interesting! *Stewart Blencowe collection*

Above:
Aintree, 22 May 1959. Several of these sturdy little tank engines spent most of their lives at this depot for working the Liverpool dock lines. Designed by Aspinall and built 1897 the engine, though over 60 years of age, still had a couple of years to go, being withdrawn in September 1961. *Raymond Keeley*

Above:
The shed is Moor Row and judging by the slightly faded lettering and number probably dates from the early 1930s. The engine, LMS No 11635, is one of a class of 19 built by Pettigrew for the Furness Railway. *Stewart Blencowe collection*

Above left:
Thornton Junction on 22 May 1957. Every picture tells a story – it can be hot work in the smokebox on a summer day! Class 'D34' No 62492 *Glen Garvin* appears to have survived a visit to works. This engine was scrapped eventually in June 1959. *Alan Blencowe*

Left:
A photograph of Class 'D11' No 6400 *Roderick Dhu* that shows clearly the great size of the 'Scottish Directors', emphasised of course by the cut down boiler mountings to fit the North British loading gauge. Judging by the Pacific tender visible behind the smokebox of the 4-4-0, the location is almost certainly Haymarket. *Real Photos*

Right:
Croes Newydd on 25 June 1961 showing one of the deceptively slender looking Great Western Moguls. Overshadowed by their 4-6-0 brethren, nevertheless there was very little they couldn't tackle when put to the task. *Raymond Keeley*

Below right:
Norwood Junction shed in the early days of British Rail: a photograph with much atmosphere. The truck on the coaling stage is being positioned for tipping into the the locomotive tender, the fireman ready to spread the contents as it falls. The engine, Class 'L' 4-4-0 No 31774, is one of Wainwright's last design of 4-4-0 for the SECR. This engine is one of the German-built batch (Nos 31772–31781) built by Borsig of Berlin and delivered just before the outbreak of war in 1914. *Stewart Blencowe collection*

Below:
Churchward's massive 2-8-0 of 1919 used throughout their lives on mixed traffic duties. Though they performed with distinction there was no addition to the nine originally built. Only a small class nevertheless they survived for over 40 years, which in itself is an indication of the degree of their success. Here No 4703 is seen at Old Oak Common in 1932. *Gordon Coltas*

Left:
Aintree, 22 May 1959 showing Fowler 0-8-0 No 49668. Many of these engines found their way to ex-L&Y sheds to replace the rather more cumbersome in appearance large boilered L&Y 0-8-0s as they were withdrawn. *Raymond Keeley*

Below left:
A smokey steamy morning at Canklow on 10 May 1959 illustrating Johnson '2F' 0-6-0 No 58198. It was not unusual, indeed it was perhaps appropriate, that the background to many a locomotive portrait should be a heaped 'mountain' of coal! *Raymond Keeley*

Below:
Bricklayers Arms, 18 September 1950. The elegant lines of a Marsh Atlantic, Class 'H2' No 32426 *St Albans Head,* is seen to advantage in this photograph which also underlines the visual affinity of the class to the Ivatt Great Northern Atlantics. Douglas Earle Marsh had been assistant to H. A. Ivatt at Doncaster from 1895–1905 and perhaps it is not surprising that on his appointment to CME at Brighton in january 1905, he should bring with him some of the best ideas from his last post. Indeed this sort of thing was not unusual, the most notable example of which was, I think, a certain move from Swindon to Crewe in the early 1930s! *Raymond Keeley*

Above:

A generation on from the Brighton Atlantics were the Maunsell 'Nelsons'. The doyen of the class, No 30850 *Lord Nelson* still attracting the crowds in the 1980s, poses at Eastleigh on 24 June 1959.
Raymond Keeley

Right:

Crewe Works, 16 August 1958. It is perhaps fitting that No 46100 *Royal Scot,* should follow the 'Nelson', especially as the design of the latter is reputed to have had at least some influence on the building of the original 'Scots'. It is an involved story, but fascinating for all that, and whatever the truth of the matter there can be no denying that both engines, in the original form, did have a great similarity of appearance.
Raymond Keeley

Below right:

Hellifield around the mid-1960s with Horwich Mogul No 42770 showing a Royston, shedplate (20C). *Stewart Blencowe collection*

4 Cheshire Lines Twins – 2

Once upon a time
I knew
a muddy riverside path
Its ways not graced
with spectacular view – though
In more innocent days
embellished with vision of vistas timeless
charmed from imagination's flight
The stuff of boyhood dreams.

Leading incongruously from the cobbled yard of an ancient mill that had once used the surging power of river water; edged with a steep drop to the river and flanked by a scrubby field that rose to a grassy railway embankment; covered by muddy pools which had so many times

Striking a south-east diagonal – top left to bottom of the map – is the old Midland Manchester Central–Derby main line. To the south of the river crossing was the important Cheadle Heath station. Sadly all that remains are the earth humps of old platforms: What folly! It should still be there: it is at the centre of an extensive residential area which has no direct access to the City centre. There was, and still is, space in abundance for a superb 'park and ride' suburban commuter station. Ten years ago there may have been possibilities but alas, now, it is too late. Running across the top portion of the map is the Northenden–Tiviot Dale section of the Cheshire Lines. Heaton Mersey shed lies conveniently to the east of the crossing point of these two lines and the complex of junctions and connecting spurs where they make their intertwine with the river. Little now remains of this fascinating railway 'spaghetti' junction.

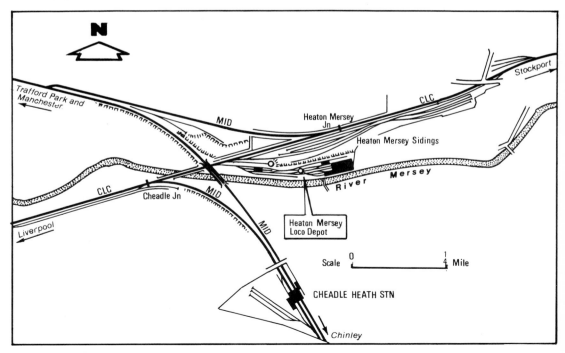

taken the impression of my bicycle tyres; time and time again this tawdry footpath compelled me to pass along its way, despite, or perhaps because of, its somewhat threadbare aspect. For indeed the river was, and still is, polluted: when low it disclosed the rotting bones of metalled ephemara – ancient bicycle frames, the twisted remains of old prams and push trolleys, motor tyres, etc. Yet these same objects when interspersed with the remnants of broken branches and river-washed grasses are not without a sad charm appropriate to the area. Alas the most fascinating section of the footpath, at least for me, is now engulfed by the broad oppressive carpet of a motorway.

But there were happier days and memories when from the riverside vantage point a wide arc of railway could be viewed, at one time carrying its own special brand of quite unforgetable magic!

Seen from the muddy cindered footpath the 'Britannia' made a spectacular sight hareing along the high embankment leading on to the high viaduct over the river at Heaton Mersey, digging deep into reserves of steam needed to battle the way up to Peak Forest. Once across the river the train would rattle over Cheadle Heath North Junction under the road bridge, then shake the dust from the station platform awnings. Optimistically, I sometimes tried to capture their flustered hurry with an old bellows camera and a 250th stop. However it has an excellent lens and occasionally, by sheer good luck, it worked. At least one of the prints does give an impression of a 'Britannia's' whirlwind pace through Cheadle Heath.

Far and away the most impressive trains to see from the riverside vantage point, or from Cheadle Heath platforms, were those few that were double-headed. Such a train was the 4.25pm out of Manchester Central to St Pancras on summer Saturdays. In the late 1950s, the train engine was usually a 'Jubilee' and additional support was provided in the form of a Compound or Class '2' 4-4-0: you can imagine the exciting visual image as one of these double-headers rounded the curving embankment on to the Mersey Bridge! At one point on the footpath there was a grandstand view of this semi circular piece of line as it came

Below:
'Once upon a time' The riverside footpath at Heaton Mersey in April 1972. The bridge in the foreground once carried the Midland main line between Manchester Central and St Pancras. Behind is the distinctive girder bridge carrying the old Cheshire Lines between Stockport Tiviot Dale and Cheadle Junction. The mill chimney is part of an ancient complex that commenced life as a bleach/print works in the later 18th century.
Raymond Keeley

out of the cutting at Heaton Mersey station, then appeared to soar, or so it seemed through an optical illusion, up to and over the river.

I would stand rivetted by this breathtaking vision – the superb outline of the two very dissimilar locomotive shapes in tandem and working very hard. Memory suggests that the piloting Compound or Class '2' always seemed to be working the harder. With a Compound the easy swinging gait of the long connecting rod to the leading coupled driving wheel gave an unfussy serenity to the forward motion of the engine, though the gruff chesty roar from the chimney top was sufficient indication that very hard work was in progress. The graceful curving lines and outline of a Compound may have suggested the elegant good manners of the courtier of older times, but that sound was of a more primitive roustabout. Glued to his tail and trailing a softer exhaust, head down like a champion swimmer cleaving the water at great speed, that most graceful of 4-6-0s a 'Jubilee' (in which design Sir William Stanier, in my opinion, came nearest to perfection in terms symmetry of line) now emitting a constant drumroll of syncopated thrilling sound. In moments the engines were through the girders crossing the Cheshire Lines and out on to the great columned viaduct crossing the Mersey. It is these thrilling moments – only fleeting glimpses of sights that pass quickly into oblivion –

that are remembered forever, the sight and sound still fresh in the memory today. The popularisation of photography gave opportunity to augment these memories by capturing the moment on film; more recently, tape equipment has become accessible to the enthusiasts to catch the sound. These recordings are only shadows that can never be a substitute for the substance, but let us be thankful for small mercies, we can grasp joyfully at those shadows!

Below:
Heaton Mersey on 22 September 1982. The footpath is to the left; in the foreground and to the right, part of the shed exit to the 'main' line. Heaton Mersey West Box would be approximately in the scrub just below the old Midland main line bridge abutments – all that now remains of the viaduct seen in the previous photograph. The Tiviot Dale–Cheadle line, disused for a number of years and partially lifted, crossed the bridge to Cheadle Junction (the box can just be seen to the left beyond the end of the bridge). Whether this splendid bridge, with its distinctive brick/stone footpath arches at each end, will survive for very long is doubtful. If it doesn't then the railway crossings of this part of the Mersey will have been replaced by the less attractive motorway bridge. *Raymond Keeley.*

Below right:
'Jubilee' No 45732 *Sanspareil* at Heaton Mersey on 2 November 1963. The Midland main line girder bridge, with bridge abutments, as seen in previous photograph, is on the right. *Gordon Coltas*

While the same riverside path gave an impressive view of the Midland main line it also allowed for observation of the Cheshire Lines Stockport–Glazebrook line. It also provided access to what, even in my time, was the quite rural setting for Heaton Mersey shed, and this barely a mile from the centre of Stockport.

Though the two sheds at Trafford Park and Heaton Mersey had, for me and possibly others, an affinity that seemed to link them together – and perhaps their connection with the Midland main line had more than a little to do with this – the contrast in setting could not have been more marked, both when they were newly built and in their old age. Whereas in the case of Trafford Park it had been, initially, the coming of the canal systems that began, then dramatically transformed the landscape, at Heaton Mersey it was almost entirely a complex of railways that changed the shape of the valley bottom. In the case of both sheds their physical setting in the landscape had been conditioned by a long shallow curve of canal or river. But at Heaton Mersey, as so often with the railway in the landscape, it brought compensations for any theoretical disfigurement of the natural shape of valley or river contour. The embankments were slender, graceful and grassy; the bridges adorned in visible strength and ornamentation. There remained until quite recently in both directions of the river at Heaton Mersey, an older pattern

to the outline of industry that had overtones of industrial archaeology. However the 1970s brought the beginning of great change and now the valley bottom is riven by the broad gash of a modern motorway.

At various times Heaton Mersey provided a home for the aged bones of a variety of pre-Group locomotives, graced occasionally by the distinguished presence of venerable express locomotives of yesteryear and particularly those of Great Central origin. A few brief months in 1950 also saw the blossoming from the ash and clinker of Heaton Mersey of a somewhat exotic plant of the locomotive world. I believe it to have been the most notable visitor in the lifetime of the shed, but more about that later.

Although the bulk of the shed's duties covered freight workings, there had always been provision for some of the passenger workings on the Cheadle Heath–Manchester Central locals and also the Stockport–Liverpool services. The latter, of course, was the reason why the goods locomotive complement was topped, for most of the shed's life, by an icing of more extrovert locomotive decoration that could be the spice of any visit to the depot.

The great charm of Heaton Mersey depot lay, as previously hinted, in its setting. The shed building itself was an unprepossessing eight straight roads affair with a long meander of approach lines from Heaton Mersey West Junction. The shape of the whole southern edge of shed and yard was conditioned by the very close proximity of the River Mersey, which at that point flowed in a shallow arc between steep deep earthen banks. The aforementioned footpath skirted the whole of the shed's southern edge but at a slightly lower level. In places it was perilously narrow being hardly more than a ledge in the steep bank.

The shed had a magnificent coaling stage which in its tiered position, especially as seen from the opposite river bank, always captured my eye. But it was anachronistic to the end, since the coal was manhandled into wheeled iron tubs and then tipped to cascade down a metal shute into the waiting locomotive tender. This method was used at many sheds right to the end of their lives and it seemed just one more facet of the aura of primitive – fascination that surrounded the steam locomotive.

The superb double stage at Heaton Mersey had twin parallel tracks leading up a ramp and through the centre of the building to a pair of buffer stops. The coal wagons were propelled up the ramp onto the stage and the coal transferred them to the iron tubs. It was thus possible to service engines on both sides of the stage. (For more details, readers are referred to a splendid work of reference – volume two of *LMS Sheds* by Chris Hawkins and George Reeve).

Well may such have been named coaling 'stages' – a stage being a raised platform, and in theatre parlance, a place of drama and action: At Heaton Mersey the wide open platforms were raised well above the height of the locomotive tender. The back drop for the stage was the line of coal wagons from which the tubs were filled; the performers were those blackened sweating humans who shovelled, pushed and manoeuvred the coal across an area framed – to continue the theatrical metaphor – by a proscenium arch. The open space was interspersed by vertical support columns of great wooden balks. The noise, clatter and dust – especially at night in the flickering shadows of lamplight – had all the larger than life drama of a theatrical setting.

The men who toiled at this most physically arduous of work were endowed fully, if perhaps subconsciously, with a dignity of labour. They were in their own way human Titans serving Titans of steel, they deserve a hallowed place in whatever is the destiny of man.

Naturally, as Heaton Mersey was a

Cheshire Lines depot, egress was to the Stockport Tiviot Dale and Glazebrook line, the junction being just to the east of the girder bridge carrying the Midland main line across the Mersey. There was quite a complexity of lines, in this small area, the two main lines being linked by extensive loops. The first of these, from Heaton Mersey station on the Midland line to Heaton Mersey East Junction on the Stockport T.V. line, was used by Midland line local trains from Manchester Central to Chinley via Stockport and Marple and thence to the Sheffield or Derby lines. The second, mainly a freight loop, connected the Midland line at Cheadle Heath, from a junction north of that station, with the Glazebrook line at Cheadle Junction. There were also extensive freight marshalling yards adjacent to and to the east of Heaton Mersey depot.

Despite this apparent plethora of railways and lines the depot managed a comparatively rural setting almost to closure, but before I say more on that subject I must mention 'the bridge'. This, was a slender tracery of ironmongery that formed a footbridge crossing the river almost opposite the front end of the shed. Slender or not, it was vital to the working life of the shed and, doubtless, earned its keep to a degree that many more ostentatious structures could envy. I think it was constructed when the depot was built because the nearest area of human

Above left:
Heaton Mersey West on 11 October 1960 with '4F' 0-6-0 No 44552 on a Northwich–Godley freight. *Gordon Coltas*

Above:
Heaton Mersey West Box on 23 August 1958. The engine, Fowler 2-6-2T No 40001, which is effectively masking the shed, was used mainly on local services from Manchester Central and Cheadle Heath. The photographer is standing on the public footpath to the north side of the line and immediately beneath the girder bridge seen in the last two prints. *Raymond Keeley*

habitation, and thus a potential workforce, was on the south side of the river. The river along this stretch runs between quite steep banks with, in places, vertical outcrops of creviced sandstone – the south bank being hereabouts much higher which helped give the appearance of a rocky gorge. Seen from a distance and in such a setting the bridge could appear almost perilously insecure as a means of crossing, though in fact it was, and indeed still is, quite sturdy and safe.

I have known some quite unusual approaches to locomotive sheds but none more dramatic than at Heaton Mersey, especially after heavy rain with the river in turbulent spate. The Mersey, though only comparatively short, is quite a mighty sort of river, making at its outlet to the sea one of the most distinctive estuaries with which the coastline of Britain is endowed. It becomes the Mersey in name just east of the old site of Stockport Tiviot Dale station, where the Goyt and Thame join each other, the Goyt having already been joined by the Etherow at Marple. These three quite substantial rivers between them drain very large areas of the South Pennine backbone and the Peak and limestone districts.

Imagine then, standing on this tiny footbridge, with just a thin layer of foot-boarding between the soles of your shoes and the pounding surge of tempestuous water, competing with a shrill of whistles and steam exhaust – two forces of the power of water demonstrated in very dissimilar forms, and, in the process, captivating both eye and ear.

Immediately facing, and just a few feet from the end of the bridge, was a narrow gap in the heavy wood fencing which bounded the railway property. Apart from providing a way into the shed the bridge also gave access to the riverside path and, since the only other foot or road bridges were either a mile to the west or half a mile to the east, was an added means of communication with the north side of the valley, especially in the days when most people had to walk.

Before 1914 and the great outward surge of the cities into hitherto unspoiled countryside, when the Mersey Valley west of Heaton Mersey would offer a positively sylvan setting, then, starting from the bridge, one could walk for miles along the winding river bank, and in the process see very little of human habitation except at some distance. it is still possible to walk this way even in the 1980s though in places suburban housing now crowds a little closer. A century before a relatively new railway would be a companion for a couple of miles, though the calmer more leisurely pace of those proceedings would be in marked contrast to the present tear-away hurry of the motorway! The Mersey Valley, while fairly narrow at Stockport, is beginning to widen out at Heaton Mersey and soon the river nudges the northwestern corner of the Cheshire Plain. The hillsides on the northern edge of the valley had, in the 1950s, a green and leafy appearance, only vestiges of which still remain in the 1980s. Above the valley edge to the northwest of the depot, the tall spire of St Johns church amidst what remains of Heaton Mersey village helps, with its 'church on the hill' aspect, to enhance further the rural atmosphere. A portion of the footpath still makes a convenient north/south way across the valley. In the 1950s and 60s I frequently used it on foot or with a bicycle as a good cross-country link between different areas of parental and family habitat. It was always a constant delight – for the river scenery, magnificent railway bridges and train movements, and other forms of industry sufficiently ancient to have settled into the landscape and become interesting. This says nothing of the abundant wild flowers and wild life that lived in harmony with the railway scene. Above all, at the beginning or end of the footpath according to the direction of walking, there were always the tantalising glimpses of the shed.

Heaton Mersey was not a shed where one could hope to find the unexpected. In the 1950s the locomotive stock – with one or two exceptions – remained comparatively unexciting. There was variety of course, but mainly of freight engines in what seemed the extremes of the power range, from the tiny ex-Great Central 0-6-0s (LNER 'J10') to the mighty Stanier '8F' 2-8-0s. The presence of these little 0-6-0s was a relic of the days when the LNER and before that the Great Central had provided Cheshire Lines motive power. I hesitate to say this but it does seem to me that when the LNER found a need to relegate some of its more aged locomotives the Cheshire lines never seemed far from its thoughts – though this provided many sights of interest to the enthusiast.

The dominating presence of early Gorton and Midland locomotives at Heaton Mersey – something which virtually lasted to the end of steam – resulted in two semi-partisan phrases of the sort that are scattered through railway folklore. The old railwayman whom I first heard refer, in a slightly derogatory tone, to the 'GC side' made his own loyalty quite clear in his other reference which was to the 'Derby side'! Perhaps his involvement with the rather moderate performance of some LMS 2-6-2 tanks gave him a slight sense of inferiority when in the presence of the more distinguished operators from that 'GC side'. He was recently transferred from Trafford Park where he had coaxed life from the venerable limbs of ageing Compounds – 'the best engine that ever came out of Derby'! His pained expression when I suggested they were pehaps not the most suitable type of locomotive to thrash their way up to Cowburn on the Sheffield stopping trains, was really quite a study. It was tongue in cheek of course, since I never wished for anything other than a Compound on my own excursions into the Hope Valley.

Any personal reminiscences of Heaton Mersey must include a mention of what, during my period anyway, were the two most distinguished residents on the shed, namely 'Directors' Nos 62663 *Prince Albert* and 62665 *Mons*. They came in around

the mid-1950s and stayed for a few years, mostly on Stockport–Liverpool stopping trains with an occasional run on the Liverpool–Manchester expressway. One's attention was always rivetted whenever these two engines were to be seen moving about the shed yards. They had an unrivalled dignity of bearing, whether the in paintwork was shining or coated with grime. In terms of sheer 'presence' all others paled, even the mighty '8Fs'! The 'Directors' made an interesting contrast to the little 'J10s'; indeed, I suppose in a way the two types represented opposite ends of a Great Central locomotive spectrum, because the 'D11s' were just about the biggest inside-cylindered 4-4-0s ever built in Britain, yet it would be hard to imagine a much smaller type of 0-6-0 than a 'J10'.

A slightly more exotic visitor to Heaton Mersey, though only for a brief period, came in the form of a Great Eastern 4-4-0. It was a stray from the 'D16' contingent at Trafford Park, though it was only at Heaton Mersey for a few months from about mid-1950 to early 1951. The engine found use of the Stockport–Liverpool trains and, very occasionally I believe, ran locals from Manchester Central to Cheadle Heath. I deeply regret I never saw this use and, as far as I am aware, there is not even a photographic record. It must have been a strange, almost hallucinatory, experience to ride along that particular stretch of Midland main line

behind such a distinguished visitor – especially since it probably had on occasions to rub shoulders with ex-Midland 4-4-0s!

In terms of sheer elegance the 'D16s' had the edge on the 'D11s', though the latter had a sort of handsome heavy weight good looks also enjoyed by their slightly larger brethren, the later types of Great Central 4-6-0s. In contrast to these later Robinson types, the 'Directors' did have a fleetness of foot that belied their great size, and this was just one of the attributes that placed them in a different league to the 4-6-0s.

I could never quite get used to seeing the 'Directors' at Heaton Mersey – somehow there seemed an incongruity. The engines had such a stately sort of majesty, while the goods orientated aspect of the shed suggested a more rustic charm. These great engines moved about the yards with an unruffled ease, connecting rods swinging lazily to appear from and disappear under the deep commodious splashers. For a brief period they were indeed the artistocrats of Heaton Mersey – the rest were the serfs, workhorses, tillers of the soil compared to a racer of the turf. Doubtless they made the sparks fly when they had chance on the South Lancs speedway!

The Johnsons, Maunsells, Gresleys, Staniers (and those others of your preference!) of this world sculptured to produce breathtaking curving outlines in metal – but it required the final ingredients of fire and water to produce the energy to transform a marvellous but inert tracery of steel with steam. Those legendary figures in reds and greens that thrill us in the 1980s, and hopefully beyond, are only brought to life by the attentions of ordinary self effacing human energies.

Imagine the ordinary railwayman of nearly a century ago tramping the riverside path on an early morning turn. He probably walked from the clustered communities of terraced housing that huddled on the valley bottom in the lea of the great viaduct crossing the valley barely a mile to the east. Or he came from similar housing that straggled in mournful grey-slated brick blocks up and over the sloping flanks of the valley side towards Edgeley. His living conditions would probably, by the standards of the late 20th century, be considered quite primitive.

The man I am thinking about was part of that solid core of simple dedicated people that was called the British working class. He would be clear in his sense of values and responsibility, clear in his 'feel' for the dignity of labour and, perhaps, equally clear through his responsibility to family and an awareness of his own intellectual impoverishment, of a need to improve his whole human environmental situation. He would perhaps read to better himself or, given the chance attend evening classes, he might have that envious opportunity to attend a mechanics institute or an engineman's mutual improvement class.

He would rise from his bed perhaps in the cold dark of a winter's morning, to dress quickly – long sleeved flannel vest and ankle length 'long john' underpants, hair shirt and serge trousers – all evidence of the need to dress warmly in the pre-centrally heated age! Then, with the fitful flickering glow of an oil lamp, he would find his way down the cramped narrow staircase into a primitive kitchen and his long day was about to begin.

He might be fortunate enough to have the use of a communal lavatory, probably yards away across a cobbled open yard and shared with one or two neighbours. Doubtless it would be very clean but if of the 'night cart' type it probably required a goodly supply of disinfectant. The ostentatious overtones of the word 'toilet' would be illfitted to describe such a spartan whitewashed plain brick box! If, by good fortune, it was a flush water closet, then possibly an oil lamp would serve the dual purpose of illuminating the proceedings and give some protection against freezing. As an added 'luxury' in an age where nothing was wasted, quartered pieces of newspaper holed in one corner and tied with a loop of string round the down pipe from the cistern, served the needs of nature.

Washing would have to be in cold water at a rough hewn stone kitchen sink permeated no doubt by a strong smell of carbolic. Not for him the comforts of heated water, at least not at that time of day. It needed the open fire in the kitchen range going sufficiently to boil water in the iron kettle, which in any case would be used for a brew of tea to go with his bread and dripping. Perhaps such primitive ablutions was one of the reasons why the characters in photographs of that time sported the moustache and beard.

Lifting the backdoor latch he would quietly leave his modestly functional home and be on his way. Going forth into a still dark world, at distant intervals a gloomy yellowing gaslight glow might make the roadway glisten. Apart from the echoing scrape of heavy nail studded boots on the rounded cobbles or stone sets the initial part of his journey was likely to be accompanied by his own silent thoughts. The quiet the more acute since most humans still slept abed, and the sounds of nature were banished by the closed ranks of bricks and mortar that heard little of the sighs of grassland or garden.

By the turn of the century the Cheadle road would echo to the occasional clatter and clang of an early morning tramcar whiring on its way, a small oasis of light. Then the silent walker would become aware of the swish and gurgle of the river against a background choir of steam, the sounds gently exhaled or urgent and declamatory for the shed never slept, the one place alive in a world still slumbering or sleepily coming to life.

Some of the occupants of the shed were stretching stiff metallic limbs, groaning at the thought of the day's labour ahead – or at least it sounded like that as they moved slowly, on track that sagged a little under their weight, towards the exit to the main line. Some breakfasted eagerly on black cobbles of coal, simmering sleepily as the life blood began to circulate; others continued to sleep awaiting the hot cup of fire that brought them stirring into wakeful life.

The approaching human whatever the rigour of his job – coaling, clearing smokebox ash, cleaning, or perhaps that most exalted position on the footplate – must almost certainly be captured by the warmth and vitality of the livid beast, to serve which was his prime function and that of the depot.

Work in a steam shed was hard and dirty but most railwaymen I ever did know, whether new to the job or after a lifetime of toil, regarded it as the most rewarding of physical labours. Possibly it was the vibration of some primeval chord deep in man's innermost being, for rarely did I meet one who would have wished his life's work otherwise. Perhaps those who optimistically toil over a rusting steam carcase in our present age, usually a task to daunt the staunchest spirit, similarly commune with an instinct dim buried in the mist of time.

The end at Heaton Mersey came in 1968, it being one of the few remaining steam depots and its demise roughly coincided with the end of normal steam working on British Railways – that anguished traumatic period which for so many enthusiasts was an obliteration of their world. For many of us those last dwindling years of steam were like enduring a prolonged debilitating sickness that brought us almost to death's door of our enthusiasm, a time perhaps when we wanted to turn our backs and forget. However we survived and after a time of convalescence our basic interest in railways and the railway scene brought the return of some sort of normality. It could be seen as a rebirth, a kindling of interest in the modern scene that began to run parallel with the dawn of main line steam preservation.

The bones of Heaton Mersey are quietly buried by a great gouge of motorway. But the memories remain vivid, the ghosts of Compounds and 'Jubilees' ride again leaping the river gap on their last lap twixt the great arch at St Pancras and the slightly smaller twin at Manchester Central.

Crimson Lake, costume, colour and pagentry – and it is all there like an awakening, when the spirit of the imagination moves!

Right:
Heaton Mersey shed, 20 June 1959 with Stanier 2-6-2T No 40089, Fowler 2-6-2T No 40001 and, behind the latter, No 40067. All were Heaton Mersey (9F) engines. *Raymond Keeley*

Top:
'Jubilee' No 45649 *Hawkins* at Heaton Mersey on 11 June 1962. *Gordon Coltas*

Above:
Heaton Mersey, 23 August 1958. Visible from left to right are: one of the shed's Class 'J10' 0-6-0s, No 65167, where tender seems almost to overwhelm the engine, and Fowler Class '3' 2-6-2T Nos 40004 and 40067. *Raymond Keeley*

Below:
Heaton Mersey, 16 May 1959. The Horwich Mogul was, in my opinion, one of the best and most useful tender engines built for the LMS in the pre-Stanier era. They looked and were both strong and powerful. No 42754 has a Rowsley shed code (17C). Heavy freight over Peak Forest was no problem to one of these engines! *Raymond Keeley*

Above:
' "Britannia" whirlwind pace through Cheadle
Heath' on 3 April 1959. No 70014 *Iron Duke* is
on the 2.25pm Manchester Central–St Pancras.
To the left can be seen the last couple of hoppers
and brake van of a limestone empties train
returning to Peak Forest. Under the bridge the
lines curving left are to Cheadle Junction and,
slightly above, is the main line approaching the
Mersey viaduct. *Raymond Keeley*

Right:
Cheadle Heath, 23 June 1962. Compare with
previous picture: here '8F' 2-8-0 No 48118 is on a
train of limestone hoppers en route to Peak
Forest. To the left Stanier 2-6-4T No 42469 is on
a passenger local to Manchester Central.
Raymond Keeley

Left:
Cheadle Heath, 12 April 1958. Slightly fuzzy at
the front end – the limitations of a 250 stop I am
afraid! – the picture is included because it gives a
good idea of 'Jubilee' hurrying through the
station. No 45557 *New Brunswick* is on the
7.25am Manchester Central–St Pancras. It gets a
good run up to Peak Forest since the first stop,
after Didsbury, is Millers Dale. *Raymond Keeley*

Below left:
Cheadle Heath, 29 May 1959, a Fowler 2-6-2T
moves empty stock from the carriage sidings to
form the 7.58am local to Manchester Central.
Raymond Keeley

Top right:
The first station towards Manchester after
Cheadle Heath was Heaton Mersey. This, and the
next photograph, complement others which
appeared in *Memories of LMS Steam.* Heaton
Mersey station buildings in April 1974, at that
time being used by a private contractor – all track
lifted, of course. The ornate and rather imposing
footbridge served the dual purpose of giving a
public right of way between Didsbury Road and
the River Mersey bank and also access to the
station platforms. *Raymond Keeley*

Above right:
Heaton Mersey station buildings were demolished
late May/early June 1974. I took this photograph
shortly afterwards when filling in of the cutting
was proceeding apace. Other photographs I have
clearly indicate that the footbridge stairways or at
least part of them are, along with the platforms,
buried in the rubble. *Raymond Keeley*

Right:
The site of Cheadle Heath station on 18 August
1974. It remains very much the same at the time
of writing, though the platform copings have been
removed leaving humped weed growing mounds to
show their position. *Raymond Keeley*

Below right:
'a slender tracery of ironmongery that formed a
footbridge' I suppose this could be considered the
last remaining physical part of Heaton Mersey
depot. Scrubland behind the bridge was part of
the approach area to the shed and was covered
with an interlacing of tracks. The coaling stage
was to the far right. (Motorway fence in
background.) *Raymond Keeley*

5 Steam Shed Magic

... night and day

Though human requirements for survival – for a continuation of life – are both physical and spiritual, there are certain bodily needs which are quite basic. Providing for these, whether the style be opulent or primitive – four poster bed or sleeping bag, bathroom suite or a large galvanised bowl on the stone flagged cottage kitchen floor – plays an essential part in the making of our varied forms of habitat.

A steam locomotive has what might be considered similar basic needs if it is to remain in a fit working state. Thus the steam depot provided, indeed still provides, all the conveniences a human expects – a place for eating, sleeping, washing and other ablutions. Locomotives, whether in the closed ranks of a straight shed or sitting at ease around the domestic turntable, displayed, in manner, movement, and habits so many of the functions that could be related to their human creators. When awake they breathe, have a surging body heat, eat and drink to ensure that a form of life blood flows – and they eject waste matter.

From the ficticious world of Frankenstein's monster to the present age of computers and robots, man has been bemused by the idea of creating a sort of mirror image of his physical life force in mechanical–electronic form. But of all man's creations perhaps the basic steam locomotive comes closest to a realisation of such a desire. Perhaps this is why we find our special rapport for the steam locomotive. It could also be the reason why, in the agony of its impending departure in the late 1960s, so many

decided that it must not be allowed to die.

The hushed somnolent appearance of a steam shed at night seemed, in particular, to underline this relationship. One sensed a pervading tremor of life and perhaps felt an intuitive need to tiptoe. Some slept dead to the world, the fire gone out of them. Others simmered in fitful conversation, awaiting morning duty at first light, a smoke haze around the smokebox and chimney being evidence of a rekindling of life. They would move fairly quietly just a few murmurs from the chimney top, so not to disturb sleeping partners nearby, pausing perhaps just beyond the open doors of the shed for a transfusion of their own particular brand of life blood. Many straight road sheds had these water columns adjacent to the running lines just beyond the doors of the main building. In the dark of very cold weather the cheerful red crackle of a coke brazier, there to ensure an uncongealed flow, would cause smoky flickering light to dance along the gaunt columns with their limp damp water bags hanging at the ready.

Out in the more open spaces of the shed yard others would be joined for an early morning limber up which might include a call at the turntable, depending on the type of shed. Steam locomotives

Right:
'a call at the turntable' The famous Inverness roundhouse in 1952: Class '5' No 44992 seen with another '5', unidentified, on the turntable.
Stewart Blencowe collection

have long enjoyed there own sort of 'merry go round' – always something of a gangling pirouette in painstaking slow motion. There is agonised squeak of compressed rails and sleepers as the heavyweights trundle back and forth in lumbering and apparently painful deep voiced movement. Elsewhere there is the clatter of coal as it cascades into a tender, or the gruesome dusty subterranean rumble of fire dropping. Hot clinkers in tortuous shapes sizzle and steam in cooling water jets, a disposal of well digested waste matter that otherwise would clog – constipation is equally a problem to locomotive or human!

Away in the early morning gloom, across a maze of interlacing steel rails, sounds the shrieking tenor of a lifting safety valve, which, just as abruptly, is silenced only to be echoed by the mournful baritone hoot of a Stanier '5' waiting to move from shed road to main line, a brief note supported by the choral harmonies from a host of other voices. The curtain is up for drama and atmosphere!

The separate repair and machine workshop was a luxury to be found at some locomotive depots and these were usually the larger ones. They were, even as adjunct to a large shed, a rather smaller building, sometimes quite separate but usually an extra one or two road sections of the shed enclosed by themselves. In many cases there would only be enough room to house comfortably a couple of locomotives. There was an intimacy compared to the greater spaces of the main running shed which, for me at least, emphasised both the grace of the smaller type of locomotive and the grandeur and sense of 'presence' possessed by the larger express engine. The atmosphere in one of these smaller workshops, as opposed the vast locomotive establishments as represented by a Doncaster, Eastleigh or Crewe, was quite magical. Inside there might be a humble tank engine waiting patiently, exuding all the winsome charm those smaller industrials and narrow gauge engines used to beguile us with. Or it might be a giant of the locomotive world stilled and slightly embarrassed – a giant appearing all the more immense in the smaller scale of such surroundings, which were given, during the quieter time of evening or weekend, to an almost cloistered silence. Sometimes there might be only one or two humans visible, locomotive surgeons bent over workbench or lathe, intent on some fragment of locomotive anatomy.

Lighting was usually minimal, filtering from a few single bulbs and spread from spartan lampshades to give a bleary yellow glow that gradually disintergrated and disappeared into the shadows twixt boiler top and roof. Oil blackened work benches were in evidence; on those which were wood topped the grain could be deep creviced, spattered and inlaid with glinting metal filings. Clamped or screwed to the thick worktop, heavy in metal and solid, were the work vices, blunted, battered, clumsy looking, the thick metal scored and pockmarked, but effective for all that. They were the survivors of countless hammer blows and the chipped saw teeth

of a generation of two-handed rough files. The knives and scalpels of the locomotive doctor in the form of equally battered looking hammers, metal saws, chisels, etc, lay amidst limbs and knuckles of steel inlaid with white metal and brass. The patient awaiting attention seemed equally as uncomfortable as any human in a similar position.

The steam locomotive, being particularly strong in personality, seemed able to impress and express a sense both of dignity and indignity, and since we normally appraise a locomotive in terms of its 'wholeness' – we expect a full assembly of wheels, rods boiler, mountings etc, every bit as much as we expect a human to have arms, legs, head and body – a part missing or changed and there seems a transformation of personality. However, if boiler mountings and smokebox door are intact a missing wheel can perhaps be accepted, but change a fitment so small in size as a chimney and the resulting style can be either an adornment or a devastation. Likewise change anything on or around a human head – a hat or hair style – and the effect can be stunning or a total disaster! Just think of some of those dreadful stovepipe chimneys which wrecked the appearance of many a Great Central engine.

In this book I have tried to note down some of the feelings that visits to locomotive sheds awakened in me and which memory continues to evoke. The conspiratorial hopes on entering a gloomy shed that some revelation, some particular gen would transend in importance all the 'cops' seen on the rest of the trip; the wider view of the engine yard which lacked the intimacy of the shed's interior but which throbbed with the pulsating life of a mechanical ballet as engines seemed to glide and flex their limbs as they moved around. Kaleidescopic memories of the permutations of classes fill the memory: a 'Royal Scot' and a 'Jubilee' seen with a veteran of an earlier

age; a venerable 4-4-0, possibly a racer from the golden age of steam, the Edwardian era, would stare disdainfully at a callow BR Standard 2-6-0; a mighty Pacific, awesome in its towering splendour seen with an elderly 0-6-0, one of those long funnelled but endearing packhorses of the locomotive world. From untold thousands of photographic portraits they seem to group themselves, either smiling at the camera or viewing it with haughty disdain – and always the supreme selfconfidence of that age strikes through the posing.

The working operation of the shed – the toil of repair, the backbreaking work of coaling – had little to recommend it. But like so many human activities the physical discomfort of dust, dirt and noise gave some sort of primitive appeal which is part of the indefinable glamour that surrounds the steam locomotive.

Ultimately, and in company with other of the creations of the Industrial Revolution – those huge goliaths the great passenger liners and warships – the steam locomotive's lifespan ran its course. They had sprung from a period of great creative energy and only ashes now remain. With a few preserved exceptions, the great majority has gone leaving an aching nostalgia and a desire to turn the clock back. We dig into this past not with a spade or trowel but through photographic records and memories.

Without doubt some of my own most potent memories of steam sheds are those of the war years. That may come as a surprise, for I suspect that many people when they think of wartime, particularly the period of the two major wars of this century, see it as a time when normal life stands still. The great events and happen-

ings associated with battle and conflict tend to blot out the daily toil and routine of life. Yet, ironically, even during the globally shattering events of World War 2 there were long periods when the fires of war became dull embers, but the cooking, shopping, schooling – the day-to-day job of running the nation – continued. Factories produced tanks and aircraft but others produced the means to keep house and home together. Within the confines of rationing, restrictions and general shortages and the fact that Britain was almost an armed camp, the majority of people made efforts to live life to as near peacetime civilised standards as possible. The fortunate helped the unfortunate especially in the more harrowing times like the Blitz in London.

The praise and sentiments afforded the Londoners during the bombing apply equally to those who laboured at the focal points of Britain's arteries – the steam locomotive depots. If ever a medal was deserved it was by those stalwarts who sweated night and day to prevent the vital railway system from grinding to a halt. Many of those who carried out these duties, sometimes in quite intolerable conditions, would also be involved in other energy-consuming tasks like air raid warden or home guard duties.

As the war progressed the burden of work in the steam depots intensified. Though passenger timetables were slimmed down, they still represented a staggering number of services. Added to those were the troop and other special trains plus a huge increase in goods train working. It was perhaps one of the miracles of the war that despite the number of services and the interruptions caused by air raids, particularly in the large towns and London, there were few major breakdowns in services.

In those days it was referred to in the press and on the wireless (radio!) as 'Keeping Britain on the move' and primarily it meant railways since we were still, just about, living in a railway world. It was a big job and railway staff of those days coped marvellosly, even miraculously at times.

This seems a good moment to briefly digress and trail that ever favourite red herring we older enthusiasts are fond of, for after the war came the legends that said this or that locomotive was the 'engine that won the war'. Truth is that whatever the valiant contributions of 'Green Arrows' or Class '5s' it was a combined effort of many. But then it is one of the joys of life to have heroes, especially in the locomotive world.

If you lived south and west of Banbury perhaps you championed that candidate for railway folklore, the splendid Great Western 'Castles' – they were good at winning as other East and West Coast giants had discovered. You perhaps had an afterthought that the 'Halls' shouldn't be forgotten: they were well and truly on the ball and could, and did handle with superb reliability, anything from the heaviest passenger trains, and still sweat it out with the best 2-8-0s in the business of heavy freight.

Admittedly whenever you travelled on the LMS in wartime there was an impression that the Class '5s', though in fact a comparatively new type, had become ubiquitous. They were just about everywhere, giving proof of the validity of the description 'Pocket Hercules' endowed them by admiring footplate staff. In terms of performance they were constantly proving that whatever had been done before, even by the best of pre- and post-Group engines, they could do better. Without the go anywhere '5s' the wartime record of the LMS might have been less impressive. Indeed, it is interesting to speculate what sort of state the LMS might have been in to operate through almost six years of war – something that would have tested the best transport systems – had Stanier not appeared on the scene when he did. For without question it was a combined effort of all those marvellous Stanier engines – '5s', 'Jubilees', 'Pacifics', '8Fs' etc, that did so much to keep things moving on Britain's largest railway.

Spellbound! yes indeed that's what we were, at Peterborough, Doncaster or anywhere else on the East Coast main line when we observed immense trains of such length they never seemed to end. Surely that 'A4' at the end was heading towards a sort of immortality – but then the next one would be an 'A3' followed by a 'Green Arrow': were they all in the same league? Well I think so – I saw them at it. These were efforts that exceeded all expectations and were spectacular enough to justify posterity entering them into its own book of mythology.

For reasons connected with early life the Southern, its engines, and the down-land or seascapes they saw, had become part of the 'never never land' of memory forever associated with the magic of childhood. Therefore it seemed appropriate that the engines showing brave face towards the enemy in 1940 should have similar stirring names as their compatriots of the air, the Spitfire and Hurricane. *Lord Nelson, King Arthur, Excalibur, Sir Galahad*, etc, they symbolised our defiance of tyranny. Southern engines were right in the front line and, named or not, served that vital, vulnerable south and southeastern approach to the Metropolis. But if only for the modestly efficient

way they carried that duty they quite measured up to the efforts of their colleagues north of the Thames.

My own wartime journeys had increased significantly once I had donned blue uniform, and are a feature of my two previous books. This opportunity for extended travel went hand in hand with increased opportunity for shed visiting and 'doing'. I make the distinction because, incredible though it may seem, I actually visited certain sheds with official written permit – wartime or not! At these, St Rollox and Polmadie, it became a semi-permanent invitation while I remained stationed in that area. Of course at the majority of sheds the 'doing' still required the maximum of persuasion and ingenuity to achieve the necessary permission to look around, though I must say that, almost without exception, the shed foremen I came into contact with were always kindly disposed once they realised the interest was serious and genuine.

As a finale to my steam shed memories I must recount one particular visit to St Rollox where a friendly contact named, if memory serves me right, Yule occasionally presided. He would be a man in his early middle age and sometimes he acted as shed foreman on a Saturday afternoon. If he had time to spare we would enjoy a short chat, which sometimes centred around my obsessive interest in that small but highly individual 'band of brothers' the Scottish 4-6-0s, and in particular those produced by Cummings for the Highland and McIntosh and Pickersgill for the Caledonian. Put them

Right:
The turntable at St Margarets on 21 May 1957 with Reid's 0-6-0 magnum opus LNER 'J37' No 64542. These 0-6-0s ranked among the largest seen in Britain. The engine has the Stirling (63B) shedplate as well as the name stencilled on the bufferbeam. *Raymond Keeley*

all together and they only represent a small fraction among the mighty legions of 4-6-0s produced south of the border – the legendary Cardean and the handful that comprised his ilk had gone long before time and opportunity had finally allowed me to explore the hinterland north of Carlisle. However, it was not yet too late to find the one or two notables that were still in the land of living – but time was running out and all too soon they too would be into the history books.

Mr Yule gazed quizzically at me across his ancient and massive pannelled desk. The picture in my mind shows him sitting there like a venerable guru about to illuminate the proceedings with some momentous revelation – balm perhaps for my soul. As if to etch more sharply in my memory the importance of those moments, my eyes were constantly caught by the large picture on the dark oak of the wall behind his desk. The heavy framed slightly faded sepia photograph, taken I think in St Rollox Works yard, showed some Caledonian notables, top hatted gentlemen in suitably dignified but expressionless poses, and a top hatted – if long funnelled could be thus described – equally selfconscious ancient of the locomotive world. He somehow looked very much more alive than any of the humans grouped around his person!

'Och a dinna think you'll be dis-

appointed today laddie,' said Mr Yule. After one or two visits in recent weeks the number of 'cops', if not the interest, was beginning to thin a little, so I was, to say the least, curious. But he wouldn't be drawn. We chatted on for a few minutes while downing the remains of the tea brew, then eventually he suggested a stroll round the running shed. This is itself was unusual for on the other occasions he had been on duty he had always left me to wander round on my own.

He waited patiently as I paused by each engine to take notes, occasionally making comments concerning a next duty or to remark on minor problems that were being experienced.

Then came one of these memories when for a fraction of a second one registers a suspension of belief – the feeling of discovery of the unexpected and the moment of unreality, always, seemed more intense in the darkened interior of a steam shed. It happened many times to me in those days of steam and steam observation, when something in excess of 20,000 steam locomotives roamed this small island.

We were passing the tender end of one locomotive when the outside cylinders and smokebox of the next came into view. For a start outside cylinders were far from the norm on a Caley engine. Then it registered – and I didn't need the number on the smokebox door for identification: one of Pickersgill's Oban Bogies, and indeed the one remaining survivor from the eight originally built. I stopped dead in my tracks and thought, this is it, this is why he wanted to walk round with me. I looked quizzically at him and he smiled, 'Aye, but naw one o' Pickersgill's best I reckon.'

The number 14621 is a treasured entry in my records – lovely little 4-6-0, as it was the last of the line it was somewhat elusive. Now it was captured and in the nick of time too, for it was withdrawn the next year, by which time I was baking in the Middle East sun. He was right enough in his remark of course, for it would seem that Pickersgill's smaller 4-6-0 suffered just as much in performance as the largest Scottish 4-6-0s, the '956s'. But performance aside, 14621 was indeed a joy to behold. (Incidentally, there is a superb photograph – the best ever in my opinion, of 14622 piloting a Clan on an express leaving Oban in LMS days. It is in Mr Ransome Wallis's book *Locomotives of the Big Four.*)

The shed done, and me very satisfied with 14621 safely in the notebook, he then, rather mysteriously, suggested that we be 'awa' to the repair shop'. This, as I recall, was a two-road building on the south side of the main shed, each road enclosed at the running end by massive wooden double doors shaped to the opening and inset at ground level with a smaller door just large enough for a man to go through. The main doors were closed and the bolts shot home so we stopped and clambered through the small door. Like Alice through the looking glass, there was an immediate contrast; exterior sounds were snuffed out, inside all was still and deathly silent, our footsteps echoing on the stone sets between the rails.

In a moment I knew that 14621 had been only the aperitif. One often hears the phrase 'it fair took my breath away' – if such is possible then it happened to me at that moment. The sight which met my eyes makes one of the few pictures that remain indelible in my mind. Large windows made the place quite light. Round the edges a miscellany of work benches, engine fittings, bits of piping, etc, seemed almost to be leaning towards and growing up the walls. Pride of central position, standing in a sort of splendid isolation, was a magnificent railway engine. The number on the smokebox of this magnificent vision was 14763 and the shed plate pronounced it to be from Inverness (32A). I was informed the engine

was in works for a minor repair after a running in turn, and certainly the pristine external condition did 'fair take the breath away'. The name adorning the long splasher might well have been written in letters of fire – *Clan Fraser* they spelled and, yes it was true, this was my first Highland 'Clan'. In those moments Cummings became almost canonised in my mind and St Rollox's repair shop a shrine – and perhaps bells were ringing, well in my mind anyway.

In one afternoon, on 18 March 1944 (and what an afternoon for I had already been round Eastfield and Cowlairs Works yard where, incidentally, the new 'A2' No 2005 was on view), I had seen the last elusive Pickersgill Oban Bogie and my first 'Clan'. I came down to earth to hear the words, 'Aye she's a real beauty – I said you'd no' be disappointed.' I had to hand it to him, his lead to that moment had been masterly. I assured him that it would go down as one of the great moments in my life and, after 40 years, I can truthfully say that it still remains one of the highlights of my life.

Perhaps in a wartime of blackout and a sense of involvement in great events, the mystique of a steam shed was even more heavily emphasised. Of one thing I am quite sure, my five and a half years of wartime travel and shed trips coincided with one of the most interesting periods of locomotive movements and achievement in the history of steam railways. The sad thing is that there were so many happenings and experiences that could not be photographically recorded during that time. Indeed only mention the 'Dump' in St Rollox Works yard in 1944 – well, it just pains me to think about what didn't get captured by the camera on that hallowed ground.

We should give thanks that something of the vibrant atmosphere and emotional appeal of the locomotive shed of long ago – that which I have tried to describe in words – has been captured for posterity at

Dinting, Bridgenorth, Didcot and many other places. 'Ah yes' the purist might whisper 'but it is only the shadow, not the substance!' But what a magnificent shadow! We have found a stage upon which to re-enact a glorious past, and what magnificent theatre it is with the leading players so gorgeously costumed in their reds, greens and even lined black, bejewelled with brass and copper tracery.

From curtain up to the final encore they hold us enthralled as they parade in their finery. Make believe? – perhaps, but on the kind of heroic scale a Shakespeare uses, capturing us with bold dramatic flourish as they bring alive the dusty pages of history.

What a debt we owe to the steam preservationists, for indeed the steam railways and locomotives operating today are a credit to the ingenuity, imagination and hard work of a comparative few. Thanks to them we continue to enjoy the sunset glow of this most civilised creation of man – shining on an increasingly cold clinical computerised land.

Below:
Springs Branch, 2 April 1958. This photograph was taken from the carriage window of a St Helens–Wigan local train. The two Class 'J10' 0-6-0s make strange bedfellows with the North Western 0-8-0 and Stanier '8F' 2-8-0. The 'J10s' were transferred to Springs Branch when the small shed at Lower Ince closed in 1952. It always seemed incongruous to see them on station pilot duties at the North Western station – elderly Great Central engines on the West Coast main line! *Raymond Keeley*

Bottom:
Sunderland, 21 May 1958 – a variety of ex-North Eastern engines on view including, to the right, one of the mighty 'Q7s' about to take liquid refreshment. *Raymond Keeley*

Above:
A busy scene at Agecroft, July 1959. This
photograph was also taken from the train and
shows, to the left, the front end of a Fowler 0-8-0,
then Class '5s' Nos 44823 and 44987 and North
Western 0-8-0 No 49199. *Raymond Keeley*

'The atmosphere in one of these smaller
workshops – was quite magical!'

Below:
'Inside there might be a humble tank engine'.
Ryde Works on 26 June 1959, with Adams 0-4-4T
(Class '02') No 35 *Freshwater*. I was never one
to consider that a locomotive portrait should be
clear of all obtruding items, human or otherwise,
for so often they help bring the picture alive.
Raymond Keeley

Above:
Dinorwic Slate Quarry Railway, May 1949. The little Hunslet 0-4-0 saddle tank *Jerry M* of 1895 rests quietly inside the Gilfach Ddu workshops at Llanberis. *Raymond Keeley*

Below:
Haymarket repair workshop on 21 May 1957 where No 62420 *Dominie Sampson* undergoes heavy repairs. Both this engine and No 62422 behind have the Hawick (64G) shedcode plate as well as the name stencilled on the bufferbeam. *Raymond Keeley*

'The patient awaiting attention . . .'

Above:
**'Jubilee' class No 45717 *Dauntless* in trouble at
Springs Branch on 22 May 1959. The cause of
the problem is not known.** *Raymond Keeley*

Below:
**Class '2P' 4-4-0 No 40548 at Sheffield
Grimesthorpe on 10 May 1959.** *Raymond Keeley*

Above:
No 49399 receives attention to the front coupled wheels and axleboxes at Bank Hall on 22 may 1959. The wheel drop is contained in the shed behind the engine. The engine has an Edge Hill (8A) shedcode. *Raymond Keeley*

Below:
No 46232 *Duchess of Montrose* at Crewe Works shorn of chimney and various other parts, struggles to retain some semblance of dignity as befits a 'Duchess'. *Stewart Blencowe collection*

Above:
Doncaster Shed, 10 May 1959, with Class 'A3' Pacific No 60080 *Dick Turpin* outside the workshops. Double chimney and trough deflectors, which so changed the appearance of these engines, were later aquisitions. The shedplate indicates Heaton (52B). *Raymond Keeley*

Below:
Millhouses, 10 May 1959 – left to right: Class '4F' 0-6-0 No 43882; Class '2P' 4-4-0 No 40542 (16A); and Ivatt '2MT' 2-6-2T No 41245 (41C). *Raymond Keeley*

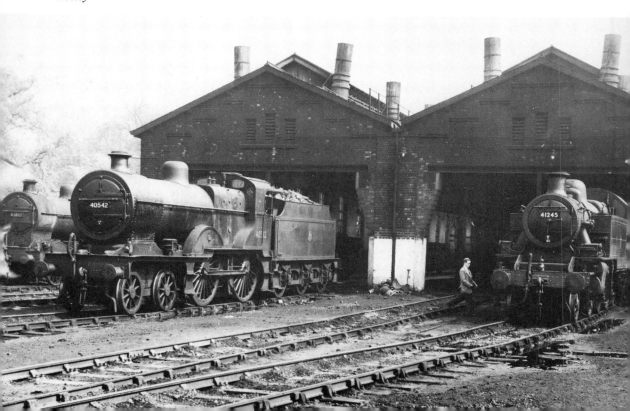

Above:
Bournemouth shed yards, 24 June 1959. One could possibly use that famous phrase 'dignity and impudence' – but which way round? Drummond Class 'M7' 0-4-4T No 30108 poses with debonair 'West Country' Pacific No 34048 *Crediton.*
Raymond Keeley

Below:
Heaton Mersey, 5 October 1958. Visible are '4Fs' Nos 44286 and 44601 (17A), '8F' No 48503 (9F) and the rear end of a Horwich Mogul tender.
Raymond Keeley

'We should give thanks that something of the vibrant atmosphere and emotional appeal – has been captured for posterity . . .'

Top:
'They hold us to enthralled as they parade in their finery.' The magnificent No 4930 *Hagley Hall* at work on the Severn Valley Railway in September 1981. *Stewart Blencowe collection*

Above left:
Stockport station on 16 May 1981. It is sad we have only one 'Scotsman' – but at least we have a whole handful of the marvellous 'A4's. Looking as irresistable as ever No 4498 *Sir Nigel Gresley* pauses briefly on an enthusiasts special at the very spot where 20 odd years before I had, on many occasions, photographed 'Scots', 'Duchesses', 'Jubilees' etc. In those days I couldn't possibly imagine that 20 years hence I could be

photographing an immaculate 'A4' on the same ground. *Raymond Keeley*

Above right:
Let the last word on preservation be 'wizardry' – for wizardry it certainly is! Here on the Festiniog Railway, at Tan-Y-Bwlch station on 1 July 1981 a bit of wizardry has brought from the ashes of the old, the new Double Fairlie of 1979. After many years hard slog *Earl of Merioneth* is reborn. While some may deplore the more 'modern' outline I think it is quite splendid. It seems to epitomise the determination, that has been the underlying feature of Festiniog effort, to project the image of a past glory, while making use of the most up to date engineering and scientific methods of running a railway. How marvellous that in the 1980s we can ride behind such an engine and for the whole length of the line, Portmadoc to Blaenau. Thirty years ago it would have seemed an impossible pipe dream. *Raymond Keeley.*